MID-TERM GOALS SUCK!

The Five Secrets to Goal Setting for Success

MOHSEN ZARGARAN

Copyright © 2020 Mohsen Zargaran

All rights reserved. No part of this book may be used or reproduced in any manner whatsoever without written permission except in the case of brief quotations embodied in critical articles or reviews.

Thank you for buying an authorized edition of this book and for complying with copyright laws by not reproducing, scanning, or distributing any part of it in any form without permission. You are supporting writers and their hard work by doing this.

For information contact:
mohsen@mohsenzargaran.com

I dedicate this book to my loving wife, Samira, whose love and strength has seen us through all of our journeys so far.

Thank you to all of my friends who gave me the energy and the motivation to pursue my dream; and to the ones who inspired me by sharing their stories.

*Special thanks to Amir and Norma,
who supported me from the very beginning
Your support, as always, is deeply appreciated.*

This book is going to take you on a journey of becoming. It will lead you through a series of powerful and life-changing concepts which you can put into use in order to achieve lasting success. You can achieve anything your heart desires. It's not just a cliché. It all comes down to your willingness to transform yourself, your way of thinking and your way of engaging with yourself. Goal setting books are a dime a dozen, but I can assure you that my strategies to achieving success are like nothing you've encountered before. Your question going into this shouldn't be: "What if I don't achieve my goals" – because you will. Your question should be: "What if I do achieve my goals and have not prepared for what comes after?"

CONTENTS

Title Page	1
Copyright	2
Dedication	3
Epigraph	4
Foreword	7
Introduction	9
DREAMING STAGE	11
IMAGINATION STAGE	37
PRAY	67
LET IT GO	90
HELPING OTHERS	118
About The Author	147
GLOSSARY	151
BIBLIOGRAPHY	155

FOREWORD

This book is an amazing journey through introspection. It is amazing how everyone who has read it has gained something completely different and unique from it.
When I first read the manuscript, I was going through a tumultuous period in my life; plagued with the stress of closing down my businesses due to the covid-19 pandemic, and suffering with ill health due to stress. The perspective I gained from this book and the power that I was able to take back has allowed me to reshape my life amidst one of the darkest hours in our collective history.
Mohsen has offered a great insight into the realm of what we call success and completely turned it on its head. The book not only theorizes in terms of how to achieve lifelong success, it actually lays out action plans to do so.
I owe the start of a new era in my life to this book and to its author, and I am forever in their debt.

- *Melissa Mitchell Sales Director at Volse Agency*

INTRODUCTION

Mid-term goals suck! You do not need mid-term goals; you just need one long term goal – or vision - and a series of very short-term goals in order to achieve that end goal. Having short-term goals ensures that you have constant tangible targets to meet, which will keep you motivated enough to continue along the journey to achieving your end goal.

This rule applies to people and businesses alike. What is the point of placing 24 or 36 month targets in the forefront, when an ever changing work environment could lead to this going to waste? Several rounds of adjustments would have to be done on those goals every quarter just to blindly re-adjust to an already blind target. It is senseless!

I am going to show you how to move from the Dreaming Phase of a goal all the way up to achieving that goal.

Before we get started, I need you to acknowledge that in order to begin setting and achieving an end goal via a series of short-term goals; you need to prepare yourself. Think of life's journey as if you are riding in a car.

The car has a **body,** which represents your physical body. You must take care of it in order to reach your destination safely. A nutritious diet, the correct amount of sleep, low stress levels and physical activity are amongst some of the ways that you maintain your body.

The car has an **engine,** which represents your brain. You need to make sure that it is maintained and that you lubricate it with positivity and knowledge. Without your engine in top performance, you're not going anywhere.

The car has **tires,** which represent your close connections. You rely on your network of friends and family to carry you over difficult roads along your journey. You need to take care of these relationships and ensure that you are fostering healthy ones.

The car needs **fuel,** which represents money. Money is not everything, but it is necessary to move forward. That being said, too much money, too fast, and in the wrong hands is potentially dangerous. Know the size of your fuel tank!

The car needs a **driver,** which represents your soul. Nurture your soul and make sure that your driving force has the wisdom and strength to get you to your destination. It all lies within your soul; just as a driver possesses the map and compass that will get you to your destination safely.

All of these elements must be in balance before you can move forward toward your end goal. A car with a big body and a small engine won't have the power capacity to move forward. Similarly, a car with a full tank of gas, but no tires, is going nowhere, fast.

Now that you know the mindset that is needed in order to achieve your end goal, and see long-term success, let's get into the five stages of hyper-goal setting.

DREAMING STAGE

How you find your vision

I want to introduce you to the concept of dreaming. What is a dream - and how can you move yourself from the dreaming phase to the achieving phase? Firstly, you should acknowledge that a dream without the necessary positive action will, forever, remain a dream. Nonetheless, dreaming is the cornerstone of achieving your goals. It is the inception upon which you will base most of your decisions in your strides towards achievement.

Having a dream is like having a balloon. Your dream is tethered to you like a balloon tethered to a string, and you can see it floating above you - but no one else can see it. They might know what a balloon looks like in general, but only you know what your specific balloon looks like. At this stage, it is likely that you do not even know the intricate details of your own balloon. As you dream, it will evolve and change constantly. Each one of us, at any given moment, may be walking around with our own invisible balloon. I'm sure you have all heard some variation of the following statement, "I don't mean to burst your bubble, but I just don't see how that idea would work." This statement is very important, and I'll tell you just why in a moment.

Due to the fact that you are in the infancy of envisioning

a goal, it is very easy for someone to burst your bubble - or your balloon. What does this mean? Simply put, this means that while you are in the inception - or dreaming - stage of a goal, you are not yet clear on the methods that you will use to achieve it. There is a high element of self-doubt, and this very delicate balloon only takes one seemingly well-thought opposing comment to burst it. Now trust me, this does not always come from someone with ill-will towards you. On the contrary, it usually comes from the people closest to you. Well-meaning friends and family members may try to sway you from your goals; not in an attempt to hurt you, but in an attempt to protect you from what they perceive to be threats to your livelihood. Remember, they cannot see your balloon, and attempting to explain it to them at this point may prove difficult. So here is my first piece of advice during the dreaming stage of setting lifelong goals: keep it to yourself!

As you begin dreaming a new dream, you may be overcome with a wave of emotions: fear, excitement, or even anxiety. Speaking about it seemingly reduces this stress, but this stress reduction is a temporary and sometimes detrimental cure to what ails you. Have you ever felt like the words in your head do not match the words that come out of your mouth? This is a very common phenomenon and can be attributed, in part, to not having a clear vision of your goal. Speaking about your dreams in haste, therefore, limits your capability to process what you are thinking in the moment and convey the message across. A brilliant dream or idea in your mind may come out as poorly thought out, or disjointed, if you were to begin discussing it with your loved ones prematurely.

At this stage, the urge to discuss your dream could become quite overwhelming, but the road to success can be a lonely one in the early days. While your close network of friends and family is an absolutely important support system, there is a time and place to bring them in on what you are thinking of achieving - this is not the stage to do that. Carrying your dream alone can be an enormous weight to bear. In the chapter titled 'Let It Go' I will teach you how to relieve yourself of this weight by letting your dream go out into the universe and letting destiny take its course.

Let's circle back to keeping your dream to yourself, and take Sara Blakely as an example. Blakely is the founder of the billion-dollar shape-wear company, *Spanx*. In 1998, when she began dreaming of *Spanx* she had been making a living selling fax machines door to door. She had saved up as much as $5,000 before she began investing in her dream - an impressive amount considering her then line of work and the fact that it was 1998! There is something incredibly important about her story. According to an interview with *CNBC Make It*, Blakely "hid her fledgling shape-wear company *Spanx* from even those closest to her". [1]

Why?

She went on to tell *CNBC Make It* that, "It was just a gut feeling I had to keep it to myself, because I believe that ideas are the most vulnerable in their infancy", and that if she were to have told her loved ones, she would have ended up "spending all [her] time defending it, explaining it and not pursuing it."[2] She goes on to state that, "I needed to be at the place where I knew I wouldn't turn back no matter what I heard."[3]

You need to get yourself to a place where you will not turn back, no matter what anyone tells you, and you have to get there before telling those closest to you. Your focus at this point should be on finding your vision, and clarifying it as you continue to dream.

A very important point that Blakely mentioned is that she did, in fact, discuss her idea, but only with a small team of professionals who she needed to help her achieve her dream. I will outline the impact that surrounding yourself with professionals – as well as information regarding your desired field - can have on how your dream begins to evolve.

You need to be able to explore your dreams without the limiting beliefs of others being cast on to you. You also need to be free from the pressure and expectations to succeed in the eyes of those closest to you. The only constraints that you need to deal with are the time constraints that you set for yourself regarding short-term actionable steps to be taken in order to achieve your dream.

Let's delve into dreaming in greater detail.

When you begin dreaming, I want you to dream without boundaries. The only limitations that we all have are the ones that we place on ourselves. It may sound cliché, but it is the most important belief to have in order for you to succeed. When you begin placing boundaries around your dream, you immediately limit what you are capable of achieving. Remove the notion that your misfortunes have limited your ability to achieve. Perhaps you didn't have the greatest start in life, or you've gone through an immeasurable loss that left you at your lowest point. These are real problems and we live in the real world, but the power of our minds allows us to transcend the difficulties that we face in reality, and to dream up a better way forward. In fact, it is usually our struggles that launch us into greatness. If you can dream it, you can set into motion an action plan to achieve it, and this is where your power lies.

Let's look at a scenario; you have a dream to own a school one day. In your mind, you have envisioned children walking the halls, perhaps the uniform they will wear, the grounds and the design of the buildings. You have used collective memories of past occurrences to paint a picture in your mind's eye of a snippet in a day on the school grounds. In reality, you might earn slightly above the average person in your field, but nothing that would allow you to save up and build something of this magnitude in your lifetime; yet the dream persists. If you were to dream with boundaries, you would tell yourself that based on what you earn, there is no way of you achieving this dream, and you would set it aside. This is the zenith for most people, and it is crucial that when you reach it, you do not engage in limiting self-talk. The only difference between the people that *don't* and the people that *do* is the ability to dream without limitations – and then go after it.

Your vision belongs to you, and you have a duty unto yourself to see it through. If not, then how else would you go about building a school from a starting point of little-to-no savings? How else would you build a billion-dollar shape-wear brand with just $5,000 in the bank?

It's true that no two people's environment or circumstances are exactly the same; but you can draw inspiration from those who are similar to you, and who have gone before you. Similarly, you can also draw the conclusion that you must be worse off in some way, and that's why you cannot possibly achieve your dreams. It all comes down to how you choose to view your situation. I will give you an example; you and a colleague may both be facing termination at work. On the one hand, is your colleague, who experiences a similar amount of shock, discomfort and perhaps even panic as you have. On the other hand, is you, who decides that you are going to use this initial shock to catapult yourself into the next phase of your life. While your colleague may tell themselves that this is the end of the road for them and that they will surely face financial ruin; you have the opportunity to tell yourself that this is the push that you needed to focus on your own dreams. Your dreams, once put into action, can be an immensely powerful tool for designing the life that you desire.

This is why hyper goal-setting is incredibly important. It allows you to envision far into the future in order to circumnavigate high-stress situations - that is the power of the human mind. Moving your dreams from a vision into reality with short-term actionable steps is a way to effectively reduce stress and turn off limiting, negative self-talk. If you can master the ability to dream without boundaries - and to think creatively in the face of immense pressure - you are far ahead of the game when it comes to moving towards your goals.

♦ ♦ ♦

I have often told a very important narrative regarding the power of dreaming, and it is centered on the lives of two young boys, who happen to be brothers. The story goes as such:

In a town just like yours, there lived two brothers, aged ten and twelve. They lived a fairly normal life, despite the struggles that their mother faced as a single parent. One fateful day, their mother called them to sit down in the living room of their small apartment. Tearfully, she told them that she felt as though she had failed them. She had fallen critically ill and according to her doctor she only had two months left to live.

The brothers were in shock; heartbroken! Their mother went on to tell them that the many nights that they had heard her crying, she had been praying for a miracle. She then went on to say that the only way forward for them was if the boys found jobs to sustain themselves after she was gone.

Tragedy had struck this young family and I want you to keep this story in mind as I unravel the Dreaming Stage. Your mind is an incredibly powerful gateway to achieving everything that you desire. When you imagine your way through a difficult situation; or even through a goal setting process, you are actively setting into motion a vehicle for achievement. The two brothers in this story had very different ways of perceiving the world around them and what they are capable of achieving. Let's continue:

The eldest brother told his mother that he would not let her down. In his mind he had already decided that he would find a job and that he would look after his younger brother. He had very rapidly imagined a show reel of possibilities and how to achieve them.

The youngest brother, feeling anguish at the thought of losing his mother, kept his thoughts to himself, but set off to find the doctor who had diagnosed her. The doctor confirmed that his mother was, indeed, gravely ill, but that there was a surgical procedure which could save her life. The procedure was expensive, and this young boy had the incredible task in front of him of trying to raise the funds for her surgery.

Fast forward 10 years later. The two brothers are sitting in the very same room where their mother had given them the heartbreaking news about her illness. They reminisced on that day in the presence of their mother. The youngest brother had successfully raised the funds for his mother's surgery and she went on to live for many years.

I must point out that while I have cultivated an optimistic mindset over the years; I am not devoid of reality. The reality could have been completely different for these two brothers. Despite the younger brother's best efforts, their mother could have still passed on. The takeaway from this story is not whether or not she lived; it is the fact that the younger brother had the ability to dream without limitations.

How you make decisions in the heat of the moment, as well as your ability to dream limitlessly, is what will ultimately dictate how far you will go along the pursuit of your dreams. You must be able to harness your inner creativity and develop an analytical mindset in order to move on to defining your dream in the Imagination Stage. The best way to encourage yourself to dream without boundaries is to take other people as an example. Is it your dream to have inner peace? Research the stories of prominent individuals who have gone from chaos to a place of peace. Is it your dream to own a successful billion-dollar business? Do your research on entrepreneurs who have gone from humble beginnings to mind-blowing success?

Fill your mental space with positivity and the encouragement that you need in order to dream without boundaries.

This brings us to the next step within the dreaming stage:

creating your vision. I have already briefly pointed out how you may have envisioned the school buildings and their layout as you began focusing in on your dream. This is your vision of what the end goal will look like. Creating your vision at this stage requires you to see the bigger picture. There is an intricate map of sub-goals and steps that you would need to take in order to reach your dreams; and we will look at this in greater detail in the chapter to follow. For now, I want you to think about envisioning your main goal. That is the key objective at this stage. This is what I like to call; dreaming with purpose.

Greek philosopher and polymath, Aristotle, notably said "First, have a definite, clear practical ideal; a goal, an objective." (4) You do not have to see every crevice and valley on the way to the summit when you begin your dreaming stage; but you do have to see the summit. It is not enough to want own a school; you must be definitive in knowing that you want to own a school within a specific curriculum, which caters for children of "x-y" years old. The goal must be specific; the details surrounding that goal are what will be defined along the way.

When you romanticize superficial dreams in your mind's eye, they remain dreams and nothing more. You have to purposefully create a model for what you want your life to look like once you have reached that goal. It is at this stage that you need to tell yourself that you are worthy of your vision. The power of positivity at this stage is what will see you through; and it is important to hold true to your dream without becoming enveloped by it. Give yourself the time to process what you are envisioning and to ask yourself why you have the dream or goal that you do.

How do you continue to focus on a dream without becoming enveloped by it? You have to dedicate time towards your dreamscape; without being swallowed up by it. In the Introduction, I mentioned that we all need money in order to sustain our lives. Do not become so enveloped in daydreaming about what you want to achieve that you begin flouting your responsibilities and lose focus on the world around you; including losing focus on your job, your family and your friends. Yes, the dreaming process can be a lonely one, but this does not mean that you have to isolate yourself away with your dream as if it were some sort of mistress. Live in the present; and set aside time to process your thoughts in order to detail your dream.

Coming from a space of self-awareness is the easiest way to ensure that your motives are pure, and that you are truly working towards your own best interests without drowning in the infatuation of your dream.

Dr. Julie Connor states; "A dream moves and inspires you. It awakens your passion. It fills you with hope and pumps your life with purpose and meaning." (5) You need to draw from this place of inspiration to ignite a passion that will drive you towards achieving your dream. If you are not passionate about your dream, it is not really a dream that will take you very far. When you are passionate and driven about a dream, you will have extra reinforcement during times of difficulty. Not having that passion means that you could become side-tracked only to end up giving up; as you navigate the valleys and crevices on the way to your summit.

Corbett Barr elaborates on this notion by stating; "Your vision helps define [your] goals by giving you a framework to evaluate those goals. Your vision becomes your why." (6) Your why, is your purpose. This is the early stage of mapping your goals. Creating a framework out of which to operate from when envisioning your goal is the link to moving towards the Imagination Stage; where you will define your vision.

So how do you find your vision? Angelina Zimmerman notes that; "Successful people create their own reality wisely using the power of the brain to create the outcomes they want in life. They truly believe they can achieve anything they set their mind to." She goes on to say that, "for every thought you have, a surge of electrical currents from your brain release an unknown number of neurochemicals, responsible for the operation of your nervous system. Your body responds to each thought accordingly like a world-class conductor leading a famous orchestra, with everything working in unison from your heart, liver and lungs performing their role with precision. What, where, how and the length of time we give attention to something in life, along with our repetitive thoughts forms our neurological wiring." (7) In essence, finding your vision is a mental evolutionary process that is the sum total of what you give your attention to. If you are constantly focusing on the negative, more negative occurrences will seep into your life. If you are constantly focusing on the positive and on the little wins on the road to achieving your goal, you will have more positive occurrences and opportunities seeping into your life.

I have already mentioned how you may have used collective memories of past occurrences to paint a picture in your mind's eye of a snippet in a day on the school grounds - if owning a school was your dream. I want you to take careful note of the following concept - immersion. In order to create a vision that is centered on your dream, you need to surround yourself with information, people and experiences that cater to this vision. Watching reality shows all day is not going to cater to this dream. Reading up on the processes of operating a school, looking at images of schools, taking a short course, or befriending people in the industry is what will cultivate the collective memories needed to continue to dream; and ultimately form a vision around that dream. The key is not to envelop your life with a dream, but to make conscious daily strides towards clarifying your vision. As I have mentioned, surrounding yourself with key professionals in your desired field, as well as pertinent information regarding your desired field is a way to ensure that you have the best version of yourself to create your vision. Once you have a mental framework of collective information in support of your dream; that is when you can begin to move on to the Imagination Stage.

In the process of finding your vision, you also need to find your voice. I have alluded to the idea of self-talk, and engaging in negative self-talk is a sure fire way to terminate your goals before you have even reached the pinnacle of the dreaming stage. You must find your positive inner voice, which is in its essence, the truest form of your consciousness.

Why is it important to find your voice?

Your inner voice is responsible for many of your outward actions. Talking to yourself and engaging with your memory framework allows you to navigate difficult tasks as you begin preparing to move your dream towards the Imagination Stage. Your inner voice will also guide you out of the pitfalls of self-doubt. Before you can harness the power of your inner voice, you must take certain steps towards this. Firstly, you must intentionally open yourself up to listening to your inner voice - many people tune their inner voice out. This takes us back to the point of limiting self-talk. When you fear the changes that your inner voice may lead you to make, your instinct may be to switch it off and not listen to it. This is working conversely with your consciousness, and it is what will lead you to a life of confusion and stress. Secondly, you must pay attention to the wave of emotion that you feel when engaging your inner voice. Does it take you to a place of anxiety? Is this because you are anxious about where these inner conversations may lead? Does it take you to a place of sadness? Is this because you have remorse in not listening to your innermost desires all along? Allow the emotions in, address them and then use them to catapult yourself.

You must invite your inner voice to the forefront of your thinking; you must intentionally focus on it; and you must actively seek its advice. Now there is something worse than having a negative inner voice when it comes to the dreaming stage; and that is having no voice at all. In a study conducted by Dr. Russell T Hurlburt across more than 30 students, the findings were that only 25% of people today currently experience a "pristine moment" [8] such as self-talk or self-visioning. A negative inner voice can be trained and changed, but you must first be able to engage with your inner voice. You must be capable of this pristine moment in order to mind-map your way to achieving your dreams.

Begin a monologue in your mind and align your conscience with the type of life that you want to create for yourself. Remove negative influences in the form of people; media; television shows; or the press, and cultivate an environment that will nurture your dream and build your inner voice's 'muscle'.

Once you have found your inner voice in its most authentic form, you must be willing to wish. As controversial as that may seem, it is wishing that creates an urge for us to achieve. Wishing to own a school; wishing to create a billion-dollar brand; wishing for your balloon to take flight. Wishing gives causality to the outcome of your dreams. Wishing and positive self-talk has been known to have an almost supernatural effect on the mind, body and spirit. Making a wish, having a vision, and then placing a purpose behind it sets into motion a series of events that ultimately lead you to your goal. Seeing a shooting star; 11:11 on your clock; or any other known symbol for luck prompts most people to make a wish. The wish that persists in our minds every time we come across a lucky omen, of sorts, solidifies itself and urges us to take action. One might say "It's my lucky day today. Maybe I'll play the lottery." This is the rule of causality in play, and there is an actual science behind wishes coming true. When you actively wish for something; whether it is unprompted, or prompted by some form of lucky omen, you are not only putting into the universe that which you wish to receive, you are also subconsciously motivating yourself to find a means to fulfilling that wish. The cause is seeing the lucky omen, the effect is buying a lottery ticket - the ripple effect is winning the lottery.

Well known philosopher, David Hume, perhaps most clearly defined this as the law of causality, and he states: "All the perceptions of the human mind resolve themselves into two distinct kinds, which I shall call [impressions] and [ideas]. The difference [between] these consists in the degrees of force and liveliness, with which they strike upon the mind, and make their way into our thought or consciousness." (9) As these ideas make their way into your consciousness, your dreams begin to take shape and the process of wishing is the cause that leads to the effect of achieving your dream. Perhaps you can go a step further to say that the cause of wishing is the fortunate sight of a lucky omen - emphasized by your ability to dream without limitation.

This is also known as self-fulfilling prophecy. This is a socio-psychological occurrence, whereby your prediction of something can come true simply because you predicted it and put it out into the universe. The actions that you take as a result of a strong belief in the prediction, lead to the prediction coming to fruition. There are, notably, two types of self-fulfilling prophecy: self-imposed and other-imposed. These can be further broken down into negative and positive.

Self-imposed self-fulfilling prophecy occurs when the predictions you make come to fruition as a result of the behaviors and actions that you set into motion, simply by believing in it. Other-imposed self-fulfilling prophecy occurs when other people's predictions dictate your actions, thus fulfilling their prediction. Let's take this within the context of Sara Blakely's stance on speaking about your dreams. If you were to express your dreams to an external party, before solidifying your vision, you may open yourself up to negative comments; which could, in turn, lead you down a path of actions that fulfill that negative prediction. This brings us to negative self-fulfilling prophecy. This is the negative self-imposed, or other-imposed, prophecy that could lead to you not fulfilling your dreams. Positive self-fulfilling prophecy can be seen as the positivity behind wishing for, and believing in, your dream.

It is thus, incredibly important to find your voice, and to use it to harness the power of wishing and the power of self-fulfilling prophecy. If you can cultivate your mind to focus around your dream, without becoming enveloped by it, you will be on your way to achieving your heart's deepest desires.

I have told you the tale of two brothers and I want you to remember this tale every time you are tempted not to listen to your heart. Listening to your heart is the next step in the dreaming stage. Just as the younger brother listened to his heart and dreamed of a future with his mother still in it, you have to listen to your own heart as you create your dreams. Along the road to achieving your long-term goal, you will undoubtedly be faced with many obstacles. These obstacles will either sway you from, or motivate you towards, your end goal. The best way to ensure that you are steadily progressing towards that end goal is to trust in your heart and what it is trying to convey to you along the way.

When I say listen to your heart, I don't just mean this metaphorically. I want you to take actual note of how your heart responds to certain stimuli when you think about your dream; when finding you vision and voice; and when making a wish. Does your dream excite you? Does it make you want to get up and actively do something about it? Does your dream scare you? It is often said that if your dream does not scare you at least slightly, you are not dreaming big enough.

Kevin Kruse, for Forbes Magazine, writes: "If you've ever had that little voice in your head convince you to set 'more realistic' goals, you may have fallen prey to complacency. There is a time and a place to play it safe, and setting your life or career goals is not one of them." (10) Nothing ever grows in the shade of comfort; you must get out of your comfort zone and dream big in order to achieve the life that you are destined to live. Your heart is telling you to reach for the stars, but your mind is telling you to abort mission and play it safe. Listen to your heart!

When your dreams shake you and make you take stock of

where your life has been going, it is tempting to back down from the challenges that lies ahead of you – don't give in. I often like to tell my audience about the principles of "fight or flight". This is also known as the acute stress response. It is a response to a perceived threat to your survival. Continuing to operate in the status quo is not a sign of laziness or lack of initiative; it is your survival instinct.

In the time of our predecessors, this complex function evolved as a response to incoming physical threats, such as a dinosaur or a saber tooth tiger approaching. In that moment, a series of highly complex functions within their nervous system would be activated. The adrenal glands are sent into overdrive, resulting in elevated blood pressure; as well as elevated heart and breathing rates, respectively. Remember, I want you to listen to your heart.

So, why am I telling you this?

I want you to understand that the feeling of an oncoming "panic attack" or a rush of adrenaline associated with thinking about your dreams, is perfectly normal. It is a physiological response that has been used to protect us from danger since time immemorial. What I need you to know is that chasing your dreams is not a threat to your survival; on the contrary, it is what you need to do in order to survive and thrive. The feeling of an impending threat, and the physiological stress functions that are activated when you feel it, are not necessarily real. This is a perceived threat, and I will discuss the power of perception later on.

When you encounter that feeling of anxiety as you mentally delve into your hopes and dreams; if your heart is racing, and you can hear your mind beginning to calculate all of the reasons why you should not go ahead, you know that you are on the right track. Push past the wall of uncertainty and keep going towards your end goal. That fear; that panic; and that anxiety, should tell you that you are on the right path.

You must show self-restraint and delay the urge to drop everything that you are dreaming of. It seems like the easiest option to relieve that state of anxiety, as you enter unknown waters, is to just drop everything you've been dreaming of and head back towards the safety of the shore. Delay the urge to walk away. I believe that self-restraint can bring you two types of rewards: direct rewards and indirect rewards. The direct reward is being able to calm your nervous system and reassure yourself that the situation is not a real threat to your survival. The indirect, or latent, rewards are the achievement of your short-term goals as a precursor to achieving your end goal.

But how can you put this into practice?

When you are faced with a "fight or flight" response to your dreams, think of what your life will look like without ever achieving them. Is this the life you have wished for? I don't think it is. Now think about what giving up on your dreams right now will lead to. Will you stay stuck in the same work cycle? Are you ever going to be able to put a down-payment on that dream house? If you cannot achieve what you want for your life without fulfilling your dream, you need to persevere and hold on to that dream.

Holding on to the status quo is not going to help you fulfill your dreams. Clifford Jones is a proponent for rejecting the status quo, and he writes; "Dreaming about doing something in a completely different way is what it takes to break through in anything including sports, business, entertainment and career. Today, if you succeed building a 'disruptive' business like Facebook or Uber, you are a modern-day superhero." (11) The status quo for you may be holding on to the security of your job, or not relocating for work out of fear of leaving your extended family behind. You have to make a conscious decision to break away from the status quo and reach for your dreams.

In the case of Facebook founder, Mark Zuckerberg, the popular website was never meant to be a global platform. The platform was meant to connect past and then-current Harvard students. The website, and now mobile app, has gone on to acquire several other social networking platforms and has totally reshaped the way we connect and communicate with the world around us. A simple idea, born out of a college dorm room, has changed the world. Let that sink in for a minute. Zuckerberg had no idea what his creation would go on to become; he knew what his balloon looked like and had envisioned it, but he had no idea of the intricate details that would grow his creation into the giant that it is today. Similarly, you cannot see all of the intricate details of your balloon in the dreaming stage, but you must take refuge in the fact that by choosing to break from the status quo, you might just go on to have an immense impact on the world around you.

Due to our "fight or flight" response, as well as other self-preservation tactics, human beings are prone to inertia. Inertia is defined as a tendency to do nothing or to remain the same. If there weren't individuals constantly challenging the status quo we might still be treating toothaches with cocaine drops, or winding up our engines before heading off on a slow, puttering drive to our single story office. Challenging the status quo creates innovation; and in order for you to innovate in your life, this is precisely what you need to do.

Lloyd Melnick writes; "One of the most dangerous, and common, biases in our decision making is status quo bias, popularized by Nobel Prize winning economist Richard Thaler. This bias in decision-making, also commonly called inertia, prompts people to prefer for things to stay the same by doing nothing or by sticking to a previous decision." (12) You cannot repeat the same pattern - or rely on the same decision making process - if you want to achieve different results. You have to actively seek information and alter your processes in support of your dream. Do not dismiss your inner voice or what your heart is trying to tell you. Theoretical physicist, Albert Einstein is famed, amongst other things, for this statement: "Insanity is doing the same thing over and over again and expecting different results." (13) You must be able to change your way of thinking in order to power your dream. Your current way of thinking is why you are on the path that you are on; your new way of thinking needs to align with what you want out of life.

Stop fighting the current.

Your heart wants to lead you down the right path, and it wants you to challenge the status quo of your life.

Listen to your heart.

The final step in the dreaming stage is acknowledging that your dream is a long-term goal that may take upwards of five years to achieve. We will elaborate on this part of the goal setting process in the chapter to follow. At this stage what you need to take into account is the fact that you must be able to project your dream past the point of your goal. The process of hyper goal-setting is non-linear. It encompasses a wide range of sub-goals and after-effects of those goals that will carry your vision past the point of achievement. If we go back to the analogy of wanting to own a school; you would need to see what the effect of owning the school will have on your life. What will your life look like after the school doors have opened? Will you be running alumni initiatives long after opening the school that can drive growth for the then-currently enrolled students? Let's look at this a little deeper.

Most of us imagine the goal setting process to look a little something like the image below, but in actual fact there is so much more that we should be envisioning in order for that goal not to be the end of the line for us. Your concern shouldn't be what if you don't achieve a goal, it should be: what if you do achieve a goal, and have not prepared yourself for what comes after?

What you need to do, is dream about what comes after the goal. How does this impact your life? Are there follow up sub-goals that you need to be working on from the very moment that you start imagining the original goal? You may have an idea in mind and begin dreaming, and from there imagining. You then move on to researching ways to achieve this goal. What you need to look at is what comes after the original goal. In essence, the goal setting process should look a little more like the image that follows

As I have mentioned, mid-term goals really suck! During the dreaming stage you should be envisioning your long-term goal and its after effects. From here, you should be working on an action plan of short-term goals that can steadily move you towards your end goal. In the dreaming stage you should be motivating yourself towards setting goals that are specific and time bound; broken down into smaller attainable goals that can help to keep you motivated.

Let's recap before moving on to the Imagination Stage. In the inception or Dreaming Stage, it is very important to keep your dream to yourself. Well-meaning friends and family may sway you from your goal in an attempt to protect you from failure. Don't spend your time explaining or defending your dream; spend your time nurturing it. If there is anyone that you need to be speaking with at this stage; it is mentors and key professionals in your desired field. Are you seeking inner peace? Why not speak to a monk; or if that is doesn't float your boat find and speak to someone who has a notoriety for finding inner peace after living a hardened early life. Is it business fortune you are dreaming of? Find a mentor that had a similar start in life as you have had and draw inspiration from their road to success.

Dream without boundaries, and move away from limiting self-talk that might stop you from achieving what you are destined to achieve. You can achieve anything that you set your mind to. You must be able to tap into your creativity before setting realistic short-term goals that will help you achieve your long-term goal. This is not the time to be placing ceilings over what you believe that you can achieve. While your dreams may evolve as you progress into the Imagination Stage, and as you begin defining them in greater detail; you should always start off from a place of infinite possibility. Always remember the tale of the two brothers and it will encourage you that there is always a different way to think and to dream.

Create your vision of what your dream will manifest in your life. You don't have to see every detail of the mountain at this stage; all you have to see is the beginning and the summit. Have a clear and specific goal in mind. Work on enhancing your mental library of information, as well as your network of mentors. You need a positive mindset, and ideas to support this mindset. Once you have a mental framework of collective information in support of your dream, you can begin to move on to the Imagination Stage.

Find the most authentic version of your inner voice and let it speak! Read up on a variety of sources that support your dream and begin creating an inner monologue. Project your inner voice to communicate with yourself and the universe. Remove negative influences in the form of people; media; television shows; or the press, and cultivate an environment that will nurture your dream and build your inner voice's 'muscle'. Your inner voice will act as your conscience and your guide as you progress through the hyper goal-setting process.

Make a wish and know that the power of self-fulfilling prophecy and the law of causality will begin making this wish come true. Making a wish, having a vision, and then placing a purpose behind it sets into motion a series of events that ultimately lead to your goal. There is a science behind putting into the universe that which we hope to achieve. It's time to tap into it.

Listen to your heart. Your head will convince you, at some stage or another, that you should abort mission and return to your safety net. Don't listen to your head at this stage; it is only engaging in a survival response in order to protect you from the unknown. Your heart will both metaphorically, and physiologically, tell you what you should be focusing on and dreaming towards. If it scares you, even slightly, your dream is one worth working towards.

Drive yourself to dream differently, and to think differently, in order to break the status quo. Nothing ever grows in the shade of a comfort zone. In order to achieve things that you have never been able to achieve before, you must dare to do things that you have never done before. We owe innovations in science, technology, and even the way we socialize due to people who dared to challenge the status quo. I can guarantee you that almost none of them could see the road to their summit; most of them could not even see the magnitude of the after-effects that would follow achieving their dreams; all that they could envision was that very first step and their summit, or long-term goal.

Acknowledge that your dream should become a goal that is going to take upwards of five years to achieve. Envision the summit as well as what effect reaching that summit will have on your life. Forget about mid-term goals; and work towards actionable short-term goals that can keep you motivated. At this

Dreaming Stage envision the foot of the mountain and the summit alone. As you progress through the next four stages of goal-setting you will begin to see how the dreaming stage opened up the avenues for you to create the person within yourself, who is capable of creating the framework for your vision.

I want to echo the effect that dreaming without boundaries can have on your life. It is easy to tell you all of these concepts, and still not have an impact on the way you view the power of dreaming limitlessly. The best way for you to see the real impact of these concepts is for you to either live through them first-hand, or to see examples of them. This is the reason why I use story telling as a way to get my message across, and I have found it to have a profound effect on the way I am able to highlight these concepts.

Therefore, allow me to leave you with a personal story about myself.

I have a cousin whom I share a very close bond with. In 2018, my wife and I were still living in Iran and this particular cousin of mine paid us a visit. She had immigrated to Canada some years before the visit and always spoke fondly of the life that she and her husband had built there.

This was the first time that she had met my wife, and they hit it off instantly. It was as if I had just witnessed two long lost sisters meeting for the first time. They bonded almost immediately.

During my cousin's time in Iran, she and my wife began spending quite a lot of time together and their bond only grew stronger. They both spoke of how they only wished that they could live closer to one another, and that saying goodbye after creating such a strong friendship would be incredibly hard for them both. My cousin has two young children who are around the same age as my youngest two, and it seemed only fitting that they would be allowed an opportunity to grow up together with the same strong cousin-bond that we had growing up. My wife began to speak of how she could imagine our children laughing and playing with my cousin's children in the backyard on a warm summer afternoon. She had this vision, this dream, and this desire to foster this close-knit bond. The days rolled on and the talk of this dream started to progress. Ideas of where we could live, the type of house we would have and the activities that our children could take part in together all came to the fore.

We were all beginning to engage in this dream and to give it meaning.

Finally, the day came for my cousin to head back to Canada. The farewell was somber, as we saw my cousin off before her drive to the airport. It was a touching day that won't soon leave my memory. This was the catalyst for me. I knew for sure at this very moment that we would be readying ourselves for change. But how we were going to make this dream a reality was still uncertain.

In 2020, after two years of opening ourselves up to the possibility of relocating, we finally had the opportunity to make this dream a reality. We made the move to Canada, and there was a rush of absolute joy and a sense of fulfillment, but we were still not at our target just yet. We had landed and settled in Vancouver - a whopping 2,700 miles from Waterloo, where my cousin and her husband were living! I knew that the universe had already begun to conspire in our favor. We had already made it all the way here. There was just one more step to making these two amazing women's dream come true.

In the moment it seemed as though the dream of watching our children grow up together was unattainable. My cousin and her family were thousands of miles away, and they had just purchased a new house in Waterloo. I had to be based in Vancouver, and my cousin had to be based in Waterloo. It would have been very easy for us to take on a negative mindset. We could have thought that all our effort was for nothing, and that we had fallen short just before the finish line. We stayed motivated that the universe would find a way, and it did. Within a few short months, my cousin's husband received a once in a lifetime opportunity for a great position at Amazon that he could not resist.

His new job was set to be based in Vancouver. At last, the dream was becoming a reality. What seemed relatively impossible just two *years prior, found its way to be.*

I won't get ahead of myself by getting into the details of how we moved from the Dreaming Stage into achieving our dreams. We have some work to do before we look at all of these steps. The point of this story is to assure you that what may sometimes feel like a far-fetched fantasy is actually a dream that can take shape into reality – if you allow it the time and attention it needs. If I can do it, so can you.

In the Imagination Stage of hyper-goal setting we are going to look at how you can define your vision and begin moving your dreams into the realm of reality. In this chapter we will look at the various steps that you need to take in order to set your hyper-goals. One of the most important steps towards creating lifelong success is having a clear understanding of what it is you are trying to achieve and then imagining yourself achieving just that. Self-motivation and self-belief are the stepping stones to success and you must not try to skip over them or skip ahead. Remember, your mind is an incredibly powerful tool that can be wielded in order to design your environment and the kind of life that you deserve. You must believe that you deserve it and you must foresee that you can achieve it. Everything else will fall into place after you do this.

The Dreaming Stage: Finding Your Vision

Recap the steps you need to take in order to find your vision during the dreaming stage.

01. Keep it to Yourself
At this stage, you should not be sharing your dreams with those around you. Spend time working on it, not on explaining it.

02. Dream without Limits
Don't engage in limiting self-talk. Believe that you can achieve anything that you set your mind to.

03. Create Your Vision
What does your goal entail? What does it look like from the summit?

04. Find Your Voice
Find your inner voice. Nurture it. Speak positively to yourself and to the universe.

05. Wish
Be willing to make a wish. When you believe something will come to be, it will. This is self-fulfilling prophecy.

06. Listen to Your Heart
Trust your heart more than you trust your mind at this stage. Your mind is a tool that you will use to achieve your heart's desires later on.

07. Break the Status Quo
Kick out inertia and say goodbye to the status quo. Focus on achieving things outside of your comfort zone.

08. Know It's a 5+ Year Goal
Your main goal should be a 5+ year goal. You should work on short-term goals to achieve it, because mid-term goals suck!

IMAGINATION STAGE

How you define your vision

Before you can begin defining your vision, you have to write your dream down. This sounds simple enough, but don't underestimate the power of putting your innermost thoughts and desires down on paper. When you write something down, you are mentally giving that statement life and credibility. Writing your dream down will also give you an opportunity to truly understand what it is you are setting out to achieve. It creates an opportunity for clarity of mind, and forces you to think about how exactly you want to word your dream. How this is worded will end up being a precursor for the words which you will use when researching towards your goal – as well as when you are communicating with yourself.

You've written your dream down and you are starting to envision it with more clarity.

Now what?

Now is the time to progress on to the Imagination Stage. This is where you will be defining your vision in a little more detail. I want you to focus on just your dream, or your end goal, at this moment.

Close your eyes and envision it.

Think of this stage as being the outline of an image of your balloon – no colors have been filled in yet, nor any shading or detail. You are the artist and you can design your life with pinpoint detail.

Before we get into how you can define your vision, let us first look at the importance of the human imagination and the power that you can wield just by using it. Everything that you do in this life begins in your mind first. Every tiny and seemingly inconsequential decision that you make will ultimately affect the path that your life takes. How you use this invaluable resource will also shape the way your dreams come to life. Now you may think that it is just some sort of fairy tale that your parents tell you as a child, but believing in what you want to achieve can definitely help you to accomplish your goals. Remember, your goals and dreams are inextricably linked. Your goals are derivatives of your dreams. Simply put, your goals are the direct result of your dreams and aspirations.

It is then apparent that in order to shape your life according to your goals, you need to take special care of how you begin dreaming and imagining these goals. During the Imagination Stage, I want you to keep your written dream close at hand. Whether you've written it down on a piece of paper, or in the notes section of your mobile device, keep it close at hand. Try not to fixate on it, or revisit the statement too often, or you will become obsessed. However, as you begin defining your vision during this stage, you will want to keep track of the finer details that you are starting to create around your dream, using a "Vision Board" as your base. Once you move into the goal setting phase of this stage, it will be important to have these finer details to guide you into plotting out not only what you want to achieve but in plotting out what you want to achieve thereafter. You will remember from the Dreaming Stage that this is the hyper-goal setting process.

Famed mysticism author, Neville Goddard, wrote: "Nothing comes from without; all things come from within - from the subconscious" (14) Goddard believed in the power of manifestation, and he is more commonly famed for the idea that nothing in life is ever by chance, but rather by your very own subconscious. In essence, he believed that your mind is the driving force for everything that comes to pass in your life. This compounds the notion of self-fulfilling prophecy and the law of causality which we looked at in Chapter One. Goddard is also a great supporter of the concept of wishing; stating, "Assume the feeling of your wish fulfilled and observe the route that your attention follows."(15) You already know the power that wishing has on your dreams, and are aware of the power of your own beliefs, now it is time to unleash the power of defining your vision.

◆ ◆ ◆

Now that you understand the importance of your imagination when it comes to the goal setting process, let's work on how you can go about making your vision more specific. Whether you prefer to have your dream written down on a piece of paper, or typed out on a mobile or desktop device, it is important to make sure that it is a crisp and clean background upon which you can begin building the details of your dream. This is becoming an outward extension of your imagination and you must handle it with care.

When it comes to defining your vision, you need to assess what type of communicator you are. If we look back at Chapter One, we notice how harnessing your inner voice is crucial in creating your dream, but it will continue to be a crucial factor in defining your dream. This is because you will be communicating with yourself throughout the entire process. You will be your own source of motivation, and knowing how to communicate with yourself will determine whether or not you will be able to motivate yourself continuously.

There are notably three types of receptive communication. Which one of these you are more receptive to, will be the way in which you communicate with yourself. Let's take a look at the three main types of communication:

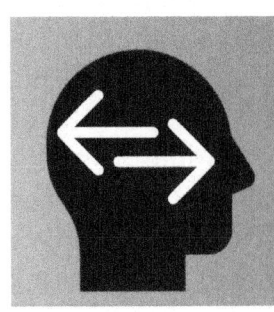

How We Absorb Information

There are 3 main ways in which we are receptive to information.

01. Visually

Visual learners/communicators need visual stimuli in the form of text, imagery and video in order to be receptive towards a concept.

02. Auditorily

Auditory learners/communicators need auditory stimuli in the form of speech, music and sound to be receptive towards a concept.

03. Kinesthetically

Kinesthetic learners need to be immersed in a particular activity in order to be receptive towards that activity's concept.

From this, you can see that people can be receptive to visual information, auditory information or information received kinesthetically. If you are receptive to visual information or visual communication, you will be more inclined to absorb information presented on paper. Arguably, this can be broken down further into 'Written Visuals' and 'Graphic Visuals'. Written visuals are self-explanatory – it is text based. Graphic visuals would be anything from graphs to charts or even pictures.

If you are more receptive to auditory communication, you are more likely to absorb information received in audial form. This could be anything from music to voice notes.

If you are more receptive to kinesthetic communication, you are someone who needs to be immersed in an activity in order to grasp the concept. This can sometimes be a little tricky to accomplish as you are still in the Imagination Stage of achieving your goals, but we'll discuss how to work with this type of communication, shortly.

Once you can define what type of communication you are more receptive to, you will be better informed to create what is known as a 'Vision Board' – but this step will come a little later on.

When you have a clearer image of where you want to go with your dream as well as how to communicate with yourself, your imagination will define your ability to add flesh to the bones of this framework – or your balloon. Before you jump up and get started with your own vision board, you need to understand the process of envisioning your success. Before you can envision your success, you have to remove all sense of self-doubt and truly believe in your vision. You have given meaning to your dreams by writing them down and you are getting ready to visualize your dreams in the light of success. Now is the time to tell yourself that success is guaranteed, and that you are worthy of standing on that pinnacle of success.

❖ ❖ ❖

Visualization is a powerful tool and it is the next step before you begin creating your clearly defined "Vision Board". Your brain triggers the actions necessary to achieve your dream when you fill it with information in support of that dream. Let's step away from the idea of owning a school for a second, we'll come back to that – it's just one example, after all. Instead, let's think of something simpler. Your goal might be to have a vacation home on the beachfront. You have already created the dream, followed all of the previous steps and now you want to begin imagining or envisioning your success.

I want you to think of the details.

You pull up to your dream home and you are met with an image of the most amazing curbside appeal. The hedges are perfectly pruned and the flowers are in bloom. As you open your car door, the warm air rushes up to meet you. The air is fragrant and ignites an instant feeling of relaxation. You walk across the threshold, through your entrance hall, and into your new open-plan living room where you are instantly met by the sprawling view of the ocean. You can hear the sound of the waves crashing in the distance and families at play just a little farther down the beach. You have made it. Think of the sights, the smells, and the sounds. Think of the texture of the front door handle and the weight of the keys in your hand. Envision these details. Transport yourself to that pinnacle. Perhaps now you have envisioned a time in your childhood that you frequented the beach with your family. Perhaps you've used the image of a beach scene from a travel program you've recently watched, and perhaps now this has brought you to the realization of exactly where you want this vacation home to be. You have used immersive collective memory to create a clearer picture.

When you envision this success, or this moment of triumph, it will help you to shape your hyper-goals. Dr. Jennifer Baumgartner writes, "The technique used to win the game, get rich, and fight illness [is] visualization. Visualization is a cognitive tool accessing imagination to realize all aspects of an object, action or outcome. This may include recreating a mental sensory experience of sound, sight, smell, taste, and touch."[16] She goes on to confirm, "As a supplement to mental visualization, concrete expressions of visualization, such as vision boards that incorporate pictures cut from magazines, phrases, and drawings often in a collage format, and small objects, such as a trinket help symbolize the vision."[17] There is an incredible amount of power in using immersive, collective memory to define your vision – and subsequent vision board.

However, once you can mentally see yourself on the pinnacle of success, there is a danger that lurks nearby. It is all too easy to begin to doubt yourself. You may feel like you are "just an average Joe." You may ask yourself things like, "Who am I to deserve this success?"

Newsflash! We are all human.

Every celebrity, every well-known CEO is just an "average Joe" – an average Joe who believed in their dreams and thought outside of the box in order to achieve those dreams. There is a method to success, and it is through clearly defined actions as set out by your desire to achieve your dreams.

Effectively at this point you are pulling what you want to happen then – in the future – towards the now. This is the concept of manifestation. Manifestation is another concept popularized by Neville Goddard. Many inspirational speakers support the notion of manifestation. Simply put, everything that has or will ever exist is present right here and now. The feeling that I had as a child that there was nothing more to create had some depth to it. Effectively, when it comes to your goals, you are not *creating* them, you harnessing what is already out there to manifest them. Your soul mate has already been born, the land upon which you will build your school is already there, the bricks with which you will build it have already been cast, and even the law that will define how you operate has already been set out. Your dream vacation home is already there. Everything already exists; your only job is to manifest it in the here and now. Therefore, that pinnacle of success which you can see yourself standing on already exists in some version of future reality. You just need to manifest it. I've already spoken about life being a non-linear experience. Now I want to reiterate this with the words of Law of Attraction author, Jake Ducey; "Whatever it is [you want], you're not creating it because it already exists. You're manifesting it, meaning that all the energy that ever was and ever will be is 100% evenly present in all places at all times and [time] doesn't really exist."[18] Once you have created your vision and defined it, there is nothing more to *create*, your "consciousness is just taking you through one of the infinite doorways of possibility."[19]

When it comes to defining your vision and being able to see yourself at the height of your success, you must tell yourself that the moment which you are envisioning is already just as much a real possibility as waking up and going to work tomorrow. There is no definite way to know for sure what tomorrow holds, and this means that both going to work tomorrow and achieving your dreams in five or more years have the same level of possibility if you make concerted efforts to getting there. Doesn't that take the edge off - knowing that the power of manifestation can see you through to that pinnacle, and knowing that all possible futures already exist in different plains of reality?

On the point of envisioning yourself at the pinnacle of success, Tom Ewer writes; "I want you to consider the following: if you truly feel that you are capable of success, then there will only ever be one reason that you give up on your goals, and that is because the work necessary is not worth the reward. Otherwise, you simply [recognize] that you have to go through a process."[20]

That's all it takes.

If you are in your thirties and telling yourself that you cannot dream a new dream, you are selling yourself short. Whether you are thirty, forty, fifty or eighty – you can achieve your goals. Time will pass anyway, but how do you want to pass the time? All you have to do is commit to the process and not overthink things. We will address the power of Letting Go in Chapter Four.

Once you believe that reaching the height of your success is an inevitable outcome, there is nothing that can stand in your way. During this phase of the Imagination Stage, you will need to take note of what that success looks like. In order for you to begin to form hyper-goals around that dream, or main goal, you need to understand what that success means for you. When you define what that success will entail, you give yourself the ability to predict with some certainty what will come after the success. Don't let the shining image of success blind you from achieving lifelong triumph after that point. I have mentioned briefly in Chapter One that perhaps if your dream was to own a school, this would be the point where you would define whether or not you will be running alumni programs to boost the level of future students' accomplishments. Will you run scholarship programs some years after opening the school? Will you provide value added services to students such as after school programs, tutorial services, counseling, or transport to and from school? This will then form the basis of your hyper-goals.

Before we begin to move on to the process of hyper-goal setting, you need to be absolutely convinced that the long-term direct and indirect rewards are proportionate to the efforts that you will be making towards achieving your goal. You must do this because if at any point you begin to feel as though the effort is heavier than the predicted joy of the reward, you are likely to become quickly demotivated and sidetracked. Even with all the motivational tools at hand and the most elaborate vision board; if you do not believe that you can achieve, you are setting yourself up for failure before you've even begun.

Managing partner at BrandAlive, Pete Canalichio, said it best; "Picture that accomplishment in your mind. Visualize what you will be doing and with whom. The visualization will give you the focus to know what to do and the determination to make it happen." (21)

◆ ◆ ◆

    This brings us to an important topic regarding envisioning your success: self-motivation. Your self-motivation is the driving force which powers your dreams and takes you from dreaming to achieving - it is a feeling of fulfillment and purpose. There are four key elements to being self-motivated, and it is important that you hone in on these in order to maintain the vision of your success. Daniel Goleman, who is seen as the father of the Emotional Intelligence concept, states that these four elements of motivation are: personal drive, commitment, initiative, and optimism. Let's have a look at these in a bit more detail.

    Your personal drive is what sparks you to take action in life; whether it is getting up on time for work or focusing on the tasks at hand to complete them by a certain deadline. Your commitment is your unrelenting dedication to the task at hand. The initiative you take is the combination of your ever-ready preparedness with the presence of opportunities. Finally, your optimism is the ability to think about situations with positivity, even in the most difficult of circumstances.

    By now, you should be starting to see why finding and strengthening your inner voice was of such extreme importance in the Dreaming Stage. Your inner voice is at the helm in guiding all four elements of self-motivation. During this phase, you will be developing your inner voice even further. You will need to be able to move from a fixed mindset to a growth mindset in order to stay self-motivated. A fixed mindset is rigid in its ways and it does not embrace challenges – instead it takes challenges and criticism negatively. A growth mindset is always up for a challenge; it thrives off criticism and uses critiques to hone its skills. The most successful individuals in history are known for having a growth mindset. They are known for their ability to adapt to change; take on criticism as a mechanism for progress; and to be relentless in the pursuit of their dreams. If you are constantly negative about your circumstances or yourself as person, you are engaging in a fixed mindset. Maria Popova for Brain Pickings, writes, "A 'fixed mindset' assumes that our character, intelligence, and creative ability are static givens which we can't change in any meaningful way, and success is the affirmation of that inherent intelligence[.] A 'growth mindset,' on the other hand, thrives on challenge and sees failure not as evidence of unintelligence but as a heartening springboard for growth and for stretching our existing abilities." (22)

As you navigate the path to setting your goals, having a growth mindset will set you up for the success that you are envisioning. Life is a process of continual change, and you will need to stay motivated in the face of difficulty. Remember that the success which you are envisioning is already a reality on some plain; all you are doing is working towards that reality. There are many different paths which you can take to achieving this success, and it will all depend on how you choose to interact with upcoming challenges. In essence, the four elements of self-motivation are intrinsic motivation and your dream itself is extrinsic motivation. In order to see yourself through to your pinnacle of success your motivation needs to be predominantly intrinsic. Intrinsic motivation is anything that internally drives you towards your goal and it can be seen as your love or passion for what you are doing. It is the pure enjoyment of the process. We spoke about creating dreams for the right reasons, and ensuring that you are motivated by a passion for - and belief in - what you are trying to achieve. This is your intrinsic motivation. Extrinsic motivation is any external source, or reward, that drives you towards your goal. The reward of owning a school, for example, or the financial gain received from it, is an extrinsic motivator.

I have held several high-profile positions in my time, and believe me when I say, if you are not intrinsically motivated towards your daily efforts, no amount of money or extrinsic motivator, can make up for that. You need to be internally motivated, enjoy what you are doing, have a growth mindset and believe that you will succeed before you set out on your goal-setting process. This positivity and drive will allow you to find opportunity even in the most challenging situations.

◆ ◆ ◆

It is the moment you have been itching to get to. Something tangible which will officially begin the hyper-goal setting process: you can create your vision board. This is where you would begin collating images of the beach or of the school or of any physical element of your own dream. Pair this with information and words that depict your intrinsic motivation. You can use your imagination to its fullest extent when you create your vision board.

Traditionally, a vision board is a physical collection of words and imagery that you would have displayed somewhere in which you can see it each day. I would like you to move away from the notion of viewing your vision board daily because you can become consumed by your goal. I will tell you just how to avoid this in Chapter Four.

Let's circle back to the traditional plotting of a vision board. Customarily, the words and images on your vision board are cultivated to create a feeling of inspiration and motivation towards your goals.

So how do you create a vision board if you are an auditory or a kinesthetic communicator?

If you are more inclined to take on information in an audio form, you will want to create an audio catalogue of information that supports your dream. We live in a wonderful technological age, where the internet is an abundant source of information in all forms. Podcasts, music and audio books are a great way to keep yourself motivated towards your goal. But how do you plot your own vision into this format? There is an effortless way to do this. You can download a wide range of applications, such as Voice Recorder – available on Google Play - which you can use to record your thoughts in a weekly journal. From here you can review and delete any information that does not add to the process of imagining your goal. You can play your defined vision back to yourself occasionally on the trip to work to remind yourself of the goals that you are setting into motion.

If you are a kinesthetic communicator, you will want to immerse yourself in activities which are centered around your dream. In the case of wanting to own a school, you may want to attend school open days, seminars, or mainstream-education based workshops. In absorbing what you hear and see during these immersive activities, you can build a framework under which you can define your vision.

According to an article for *Inc.* by Molly St. Louis; "Approximately 65 percent of the population [are] visual learners."[23] You could likely fall into this category, and this is why although it was mentioned first, I have left it until last to define. When creating your vision board, a great way to interpret what is in your mind is to put it on paper. Being able to physically see the evolution of your dreams, and how you define them, can be a great source of motivation. It can further help you to weed out ideas that may not necessarily boost your vision. Let's have a look at how you can create your own vision board.

First, I want you to write down the emotions that come to mind when you think about your dream. Does it bring you joy and excitement? Does it bring you fear and anxiety? Then, I want you to write down the following statement: "My feelings towards my goal define the magnitude of my goal. Anxiety should not stop me from achieving my goal. Fears are perceived ideas towards the uncertainty of trying something new. They cannot stop me from achieving what my heart desires."

Secondly, I want you to write down everything that brings you happiness in your life. How do you think your dream will help to amplify the joy that these bring you? If you enjoy spending quality time with your family, will your dream eventually lead you to a place where you have more control over your time? This will be one of the first steps in hyper-goal setting; or envisioning your life past the point of achieving your goal.

This links to the third step in creating your vision board. What are your values? Do you value creativity, adventure, good health? Now I want you to think about how your vision falls in line with your core values, and how you can alter it to always stay in line with those values. Remember that when you work against the current, and do not listen to your heart and values, you are setting yourself up for long term stress. Intrinsic motivation is what will help you stay the course, and your core values are intrinsic motivators. Write your values down and draw links between them and the details of your vision.

In the fourth step of defining your vision on your vision board, you will need to draw out or write out the details of your vision. Let's use the school as an example once again. Start imagining the details of the school. How many children do you want enrolled? How many grades should there be? What roles and staff will there be? What type of curriculum will you be running? This is the stage where you will clearly define your vision, but not how you get there –this will come later on. In essence this can be seen as defining your dream in some detail, but not with all the details of how to get there.

Now comes the fun part. You can choose to have this vision board drawn out on paper or via a web application such as My Vision Board. Use colors that simultaneously motivate and calm you. You can hand write all of these concepts down or you can cut images from magazines or print them off the internet. As you navigate towards achieving your goal being able to occasionally come back to this vision board, to reminisce on the feelings you had while creating it, will keep you motivated in moments of difficulty. Reflect on your vision board from time to time and assess whether you are keeping in line with your dreams and values.

◆ ◆ ◆

You've written down your dream with detail. Your balloon now has a color, a texture, a shape and a size. Now you will begin hyper-goal setting.

But what is hyper-goal setting and how does it differ from traditional goal setting?

In the traditional approach of goal setting, you would write down an action plan all the way up until your goal. That is where your planning process would end. The focus is predominantly on the process leading up to achieving your dream, or reaching your goal. Hyper-goal setting involves envisioning past the point of achievement. Your vision gets defined even further as you take on the notion that the most important phase of achieving your goal is not the goal itself, but what takes place after you have achieved it. This is important for two reasons. Firstly, if you are only seeing yourself up until the point of achieving your dream, you are creating a space in which you can plateau and begin to go into decline once you reach that goal. You need to acknowledge that achieving your goal is only the first step on the road to lifelong success - it opens the door for everything else to follow. Secondly, with a number of hyper-goals surrounding your dream you multiply your extrinsic motivators, which can work harmoniously with your intrinsic motivators.

As I mentioned, you will be occasionally reviewing your vision board, and this will be your first revision, or addition. I want you to think clearly about what is going to happen in the five years after you have reached your goal.

Let's get back to the school. The school doors have officially opened. You have enrolled some students. You have a great team of staff and an excellent curriculum in place. So what's next? You might want to consider the marketing initiatives that you will be taking in order to attract more students. You might also look at your parent-teacher engagement. What role will governing bodies, student governance and PTA be playing? How will you be offering school tours – virtually; in person; both? Is your application process efficient? Will you be offering boarding facilities for students, if you have international ambitions? How will you go about building these facilities? Have you demarcated space on your commercial plot for these facilities? Perhaps you had only envisioned an elementary school. Will you be expanding within those five years after opening? Will you be opening a middle school and high school to receive the students enrolled at your elementary school?

You can see how important it is to envision after the point of achieving your goal. If you don't do that, you might only factor the elementary school into your design. What would this mean for you? This would mean that parents would potentially have to move their children to another institution for middle school and then high school. After a few short years, word would spread that your school is not worth the effort, as children have to be moved to another school in order to carry on their middle and high schooling journey. At this point if you haven't demarcated an area to build your middle and high school, you could find yourself sitting with remaining land area which is not sufficient enough to achieve expansion. Even if the land area is sufficient enough, you could find that building codes won't permit you to build to the scale which is needed on the remaining portion. You have thus failed to foresee a probable outcome of achieving your goal and have put yourself in a position of reaching a dead end with your goal. This is why I place an incredible amount of significance on seeing far past the point of achievement. I will reiterate the fact – the question shouldn't be, 'what if I don't accomplish my goal?' The question should be - 'what if I do accomplish my goal and have not prepared myself for what comes after?'

So how does this affect your balloon? Your balloon is now going to have some company up on its string. These hyper-goals that surround your dream will become like smaller balloons that make up a bouquet in your hand. They are there as a support structure for your dream, and when they are all tied together they form the big picture for your lifelong success. The problem with the traditional method of goal setting is that you will often have a bunch of goals floating around that have no link to each other. Having to hold on to multiple different strings, attached to multiple different balloons can become quite the circus act. Think of it, if you will, as heading out for target practice. Shooting at one clearly defined target is far easier than having to aim at multiple loosely defined targets that don't even bare any similarity to one another. In short, you become overwhelmed by a plethora of goals instead of focusing on one main goal and the sub-goals that form after it.

Hyper-goal setting alleviates this problem by providing yourself with one main goal or dream to focus on, and then filling in the empty space around it with goals that should come after achieving your main goal. They work together, synchronously, instead of independently of each other.

If you are able to imagine your life long past the point of your core goal, it becomes clearer that this core goal was merely a major milestone on the journey to creating lifelong success. It is the starting point for all future successes. You will need to utilize the tools brought to you in Chapter One in order to form the post-milestone hyper-goals. Remember to listen to your heart and your inner voice, and to dream without boundaries. Don't sell yourself short. If you can harness the power of your imagination to create a framework of hyper-goals, then you immediately remove the faux ceiling which may have limited you in the past. As I mentioned, we live in an incredibly complex, non-linear world. In order to achieve your goals and live a happy and fulfilled life, you need to think in a non-linear way.

So what is the purpose of setting these long-term hyper-goals?

Lyn Christian said it best; "There's a reason that [*what are your long-term goals*] is such a common question in job interviews, family dinners, and even first dates. Long term goals say a lot about who you are, where you're going, and what you value. They are the big dreams that give your life direction and purpose."(24)

So what does this mean in terms of hyper-goal setting?

The hyper-goals that come after the accomplishment of your core goal will, ultimately, determine the ways in which you go about achieving your core goal. In essence, you are working your way backwards from a point in the future that represents the impact which the core goal will have had on your life. Your hyper-goals are going to define the person that you evolve into in order to achieve them. I have already stated that in order to achieve things that you have never achieved before, you need to be willing to do things that you have never done before – but you also have to be willing to become the version of yourself that is necessary to achieve your dream. You need to be willing to level up, so to speak. You need to be willing to fill the shoes of the person whom is capable of achieving greatness. That person is already you - just a heightened and more enlightened version of you. The processes prior to this, including finding your inner voice, represents your evolution into the version of yourself that is ready to take on the challenges which going after your goals will bring you.

Christian further goes on to elaborate that long-term goals can be broken down into three main types of goals, namely: career goals, financial goals and personal goals. Career goals can be seen as wanting to own a school. Financial goals can be seen as wanting to buy a vacation home. Personal goals can be seen as wanting to travel the world. She states; "Life has many types of goals, big and complex enough to require planning, persistence, and accountability over a long period of time."(25)

We have focused quite heavily on career and financial goals, but can this hyper-goal setting process be applied to personal goals? The answer is, absolutely! Let's take wanting to travel the world as an example. You set out to travel across an extensive part of the globe at your five year mark. You achieve this goal, but then what comes after you've reached this momentous milestone? Do you call it a day, and head back to the doldrums?

Not if you've set hyper-goals.

Your hyper-goals concerning circumnavigating big blue

could include wanting to document your travels thereafter by writing a book or putting together a pictorial book of your most prominent images which you managed to snap along your journey. They could include wanting to maintain a network, or certain sense of connectedness, to the people whom you met along the way. From this you may want to organize a reunion with each one of these people at specific intervals. You may even decide that your wandering heart would want to settle down in one of the countries that you have traveled to. In this case travelling the world is what allowed your free spirit to find its new forever home.

You might want to know if these hyper-goals can be applied to finding your soul mate.

Yes, and yes again!

We all have a certain understanding of what we want out of life – whether or not we want children, and if so how many. Where we would like to live and even where and when we would like to retire are all thoughts that have crossed our minds in some way or another. For many of us these are loose images in our minds. We haven't set concrete dates around which we would like to achieve these goals. Now, I must mention that when it comes to hyper-goal setting for this deep level of your personal life, it is not always easy. This is mainly due to the fact that you cannot create your ideal partner out of thin air, and if you are trying to do so - or if you are trying to change someone that is already in your life to fit the shape of this mental ideal – you have already set yourself up for heartache.

Instead, your hyper-goals should be giving you a deeper understanding into what you are looking for in a soul mate, and not how to change someone that is already in your life. Remember, your goals and dreams guide **you**, not anyone else. Therefore, you cannot use your own ideals to alter someone else's life path. Your goals will always be tied closely to your core values, and deviating from your core values is what leads to a life of stress and confusion. Therefore, if your goals are to have a big family with your soul mate one day because you have strong family values, then settling down with someone who has opposing goals will create this stress and confusion. If a big family is what you envision, you know that you are looking for someone that is willing to create this family with you – not because you dictate it, but because it is something that they want out of life as well. This is the one exception to the rule – *'Keep it to yourself'*. You should definitely be sharing your core values and life-goals with a potential life partner, because they are intricately part of that dream. There is someone out there who is suited to you and whose core values and goals will align with your own.

Now, I am no relationship expert, but I have had my fair share of ups and downs in my own personal life. What I can tell you with absolute certainty is this – you will spend your entire life chasing immaterial and fleeting versions of 'happiness' if you are not fulfilled within your personal life. Teresa Newsome for Bustle, writes; "Love changes everything, even our goals. We've all seen or felt the way a new relationship gives partners tunnel vision and makes them forget the rest of the world. It's OK for a little while, but if you're not careful, before you know it, your relationship will sidetrack your goals in ways you might not even realize." (26) In terms of your personal goals, it can become quite easy for you to forget the fact that you want a big family, or that you would like to retire on the coast. This could be simply because you've been swept up in the arms of infatuation with you partner – who does not want those things out of life. It is, therefore, important to acknowledge that although everyone comes into your life for a reason, in the grand scheme of things, not everyone is meant to stay.

This is not to say that you should sacrifice the people that you love in the pursuit of your dreams or vice versa. What I mean is this – when you have the right people on your team, you won't have to.

The crucial factor here is to develop the power of foresight. You should be able to predict with at least a bit of accuracy what your dream and following hyper-goals will entail for your life. It is then up to you to decide whether or not your environment, and those in it, are conducive to that dream. If they are not, can your dream be altered by using the technique of dreaming without boundaries? These are all decisions that you will be faced with in going forward with your hyper-goal setting and this is why you need to have a very clear image of what you are trying to achieve and why.

❖ ❖ ❖

The final step in setting your hyper-goals is to acknowledge that you are creating a movie, not a snapshot. The cumulative images that you have created in your mind regarding your core goal and the goals to follow will be the scenes of your movie.

Let's take a little more of a personal approach to this.

My dream for the longest time has been to write a book that would inspire others to live their lives to their fullest potential. That is my core goal. My hyper-goals surrounding this goal included getting published, reaching a good volume of readers, creating talks around my book's topic, and eventually being able to do a book tour. Having the foresight of my hyper-goals determined whether or not I would be writing a fiction or non-fiction, which category or niche I would be writing in and so on. As you can see, predicting with some certainty what hyper-goals would come after my core goal, has allowed me to refine my core goal.

I'm going to walk you through some concepts that will allow you to create your show reel, before we move on to the next stage. Up until now, your balloon has been a static image in your mind. You have given it some definition but you have not yet brought it to life fully. You have started to set your hyper-goals, and these have become several more static images that surround the image of your primary balloon. You have the footage, but your life is now on the cutting room floor and you are the master editor. It is time to combine these images and design your movie. Allow me to put this into context for you. A movie under edit has several timestamps throughout, working to give the editor an idea of where to apply certain changes seamlessly by calling on the necessary timestamp. You now have the immense task ahead of you applying timestamps to your hyper-goals. You have already told yourself that these goals should happen within the five years that follow the achievement of your core goal, but you need to define the chronology of these events. Once you have done this, you have created your movie, or show reel of your balloons.

In essence, each goal should lead to the next one and the next one after that, in a chain of events. By putting your goals together in this fashion, you are able to make sense of them. You are able to assess which goal should come first and which should follow immediately after. You wouldn't start watching a movie halfway through, would you? Let's look back at the school as an easy example. You wouldn't plan to build the high school before building the middle school. It would make no sense financially or chronologically. You know that the children that are enrolled with you for their elementary years will need to progress to middle school before high school. You, therefore, know the order in which your "movie" or hyper-goals should play out.

Steven Handel writes, "Foresight is our ability to accurately predict future outcomes. It is a long-term, 'bigger picture' view of how certain events will unfold over a period of time – and how we can act to influence certain outcomes in our lives."(27) In creating your movie around your balloons, foresight will be the strongest tool in your arsenal. You will remember that I spoke of immersing yourself in information – as well as surrounding yourself with people – which will help to form a mental framework under which you will create and define your goals. Here is exactly where the relevance of this becomes apparent.

Handel goes on to state that, "According to a study published in Neuropsychology, both past and future thinking activate many of the same regions of the brain. Researchers say this confirms the idea that our memories and past experiences play an important role in imagining future events."(28) If you had been immersing yourself in information that was in support of your goals, it would have honed your ability to use your foresight to inform you of how and when your hyper-goals should take place. As you are aware by now, attaining lifelong success is not a random act. It is only attained through a clear vision and, more often than not, drastic changes to the way you think and engage with the world around you.

Your mental movie should also be divided into 'scenes'. Your core goal is your opening scene. This grabs your audience – in this case your own psyche – and informs them of what is to be expected. The scenes that follow represent your hyper-goals. This is the sequence of events that you should be envisioning in order to inform yourself of how you will introduce your movie – or how you will clearly define your core goal. Just as with the making of any movie, you are also going to be engaging in a lot of editing when creating your hyper-goal reel. Chronological sequencing, the nature of each 'scene', and the context will all be changing during this time. You will undergo your second and perhaps even your third revision to your vision board during this phase of the Imagination Stage. It is important not to get discouraged as you unravel the process. Allow your core values and your goals to inform your decision making process. Just be certain that when the director yells cut, you have lived a life that you can look back on and feel as though you had given it your all.

◆ ◆ ◆

Let's briefly recap the Imagination Stage of hyper-goal setting. Before you can begin defining your vision, you have to write your dream down. Be sure not to underestimate the power of putting your aspirations down on paper. When you write something down, you are mentally giving that statement life. Writing your dream down will also give you an opportunity to truly understand what it is you are setting out to achieve.

It is an opportunity for clarity that should not be missed. How this is worded will end up being a precursor to the words that you will use when communicating with yourself. From here you will work on making your vision more specific. Whether you prefer to have your dream written down on a piece of paper, or typed out on a mobile or desktop device, it is important to make sure that it is a crisp and clean background upon which you can begin building the details of your dream. This is becoming an outward extension of your imagination and you must handle it with care.

When it comes to defining your vision, you need to assess what type of communicator you are. Harnessing your inner voice will continue to be a crucial factor in defining your dream. This is because you will be communicating with yourself throughout the entire process. You will be your own source of motivation, and knowing how to communicate with yourself will determine whether or not you will be able to motivate yourself continuously. There are notably three types of receptive communication – visual, auditory and kinesthetic.

See yourself on the pinnacle of success. However, once you can mentally see yourself there, don't begin to doubt yourself. You may feel like you are "just an average Joe." You may ask yourself things like, "Who am I to deserve this success?" Remember that every celebrity and every well-known CEO is just an average Joe who believed in their dreams and thought outside of the box in order to achieve those dreams. There is a method to success, and it is through clearly defined actions as set out by your desire to achieve your dreams.

This desire to achieve is compounded by your self-motivation, which will be the driving force that powers your dreams and takes you from dreaming to achieving. It is a feeling of fulfillment and purpose. There are four key elements to being self-motivated: personal drive, commitment, initiative, and optimism. Your personal drive is what sparks you to take action in life; whether it is getting up on time for work or focusing on the tasks at hand to complete them by the deadline. Your commitment is your unrelenting dedication to the task at hand. The initiative you take is the combination of your ever-ready preparedness with the presence of opportunities. Your optimism is the ability to think about situations with positivity, even in the most difficult of circumstances.

Enjoy the process of creating your Vision Board. Use colors that simultaneously motivate and calm you. You can hand write everything down or you can cut images from magazines or print them off the internet. As you navigate towards achieving your goal being able to come back to this vision board from time to time will keep you motivated in moments of difficulty. Reflect on your vision board regularly and assess whether you are keeping in line with your dreams and values.

Finally, get ready to set some hyper-goals. In the traditional approach of goal setting, you would write down an action plan all the way up until your goal. That is where your planning process would end. The focus is predominantly on the process leading up to achieving your dream, or reaching your goal. Hyper-goal setting involves envisioning past the point of achievement. The most important phase of achieving your goal is not the goal itself, but what takes place after you have achieved it. If you are only seeing yourself up until the point of achieving your dream, you are creating a space in which you can plateau and begin to go into decline once you reach that goal. You need to acknowledge that achieving your goal is only the first step on the road to lifelong success. It opens the door for everything else to follow. Note that with a number of hyper-goals surrounding your dream you multiply your extrinsic motivators, which can work harmoniously with your intrinsic motivators. Your intrinsic motivators will be your greatest source of motivation and will be the ones which hold you steady on your path to lifelong success. When all is said and done, all of your self-motivation should be deeply tied to your inner core values to ensure that you always stay the course towards your goals.

◆ ◆ ◆

I have another story for you, before we move on to the next stage. *This is a story about a friend of mine by the name of Shahram. He had graduated in the year 2003 and he began looking for full-time work. He had searched through the newspapers, sending his resume to every listed opening he could find. He mailed his resume to companies which he thought might take him on; but by the summer of 2003 – months after completing his degree – he still had no luck. You see Shahram was in a bit of a tough situation, financially. At the time he couldn't put together the necessary funds to pay the required graduation fee. His degree, although complete, was not released to him because of this seemingly minor setback.*

He was down on his luck and the strain of not being able to find sustainable work was beginning to take a toll on his mental health. The summer rolled on and his cousin, whom was living abroad in France at the time, came back to Iran to visit the family. There was a massive celebration at his uncle's house to welcome his cousin home. The misfortune of Shahram's financial situation meant that he didn't have suitable clothes to attend the party, and he felt that he was too down and embarrassed to attend the party in his state. All he had to his name was 18,000 Tomans – about $20. Nonetheless, he pulled himself together and decided that although he didn't have enough money to buy a new outfit, perhaps he would just go ahead and get himself a decent pair of new shoes. He took about 10,000 Tomans of what he had left, and went off to purchase a brand new pair of shoes. Before attending the party, Shahram first stopped at the Mosque to say his prayer for the day. He left his shoes out front as everyone always did when attending prayer at the Mosque. He was beginning to feel a bit more uplifted; he was actually starting to look forward to the party and reuniting with his cousin after years apart. He walked out of the Mosque and walked over to where he had placed his shoes, but he couldn't find them. He thought that he was surely mistaken as to where he placed them, and so he began looking elsewhere amongst the other shoes. Other men began to exit the Mosque *and some even stopped to ask what his dilemma was as they could see the panic across his face. Some even helped him search for his shoes by his description of them. It was no use. His brand new pair of shoes was gone – misplaced, or worse, stolen. A deep sense of despair overtook Shahram in that moment. He had no shoes, practically no money and his hope for the future was dwindling.*

He ran back to the shoe shop as fast as his feet could carry him – aching across the rough paving. Sweating and out of breath he asked to speak to the shopkeeper. The shopkeeper hearing the commotion came out to the front of the shop and asked Shahram what had happened. Shahram steadied his breathing long enough to explain his plight, and begged that the shopkeeper sell him another pair of the same shoes for 8,000 Tomans instead of their original price of 10,000 Tomans. Remember, this is all he had left in his name. The shopkeeper apologized, but told him that unfortunately he could not fulfill Shahram's request. The shopkeeper was silent for a moment, with a look of deep thought and concern spread across his face. He told Shahram to follow him to the back of the shop, and feeling sympathy for the exhausted Shahram, told him to have a seat on an old bench just across from the store room. He told Shahram to wait for him there. Shahram was exhausted, saddened and feeling lost. He agreed to have a seat and wondered what the shopkeeper was busying himself with in the store room. He looked around the old building and his eyes came across a small faint poster on the wall. He tilted his head and focused on it, it was a picture of the Parisian Eiffel Tower. It was a striking image, and he couldn't help but be taken by its beauty.

He closed his eyes and imagined himself standing in line, waiting for his turn to go up in the Tower elevator. The sun shone in from a window in the passage and as the warmth touched his skin, he imagined that it was the sun warming his skin as he waited in line at the foot of the Eiffel Tower. He could almost hear the murmur of people excitedly discussing what they would hope to see from the viewing deck. It was so intensely real in that very moment. Just before he could see himself walking on to the elevator, the shopkeeper called to him. He snapped back into reality, but he felt different. He was calm and surprisingly at ease with everything that had befallen him until now. The shopkeeper had found a pair of shoes that were in the previous season's stock marked at 10,000 Tomans, but allowed Shahram to have them for 8,000 Tomans instead. Shahram was incredibly grateful and just like that he began to feel as though his fortune was changing. He quickly donned the shoes and headed out for the party.

His family greeted him with open arms and he and his cousin spoke well into the night – catching up on all that they had missed out on in each other's lives over the last few years. He began to wonder why he was so worried about putting on a good impression as he and his cousin joked about the good old days. He went home that evening with a heart filled with hope. He was determined that he would make it to the Eiffel Tower one day too. With not a penny in his pocket, he was not deterred from imagining this occurrence – and believing that it would come to be.

Three days had past and the dust had settled on the events of that fateful summer day. Shahram decided that he would just keep on trying to find a decent job, no matter how long it took. He would remain committed to his vision. That very day, he came across a placement advert for a field engineer with an international company which had a new oil and gas project in the south of Iran. He had nothing to lose, and he hurriedly sent his resume off. Just one short month later, he was called for an interview with that very same company. Hands trembling, he prepared himself for the interview, and for some reason on that particular day he kept envisioning the day in the shoe shop. He recalled the poster of the Eiffel Tower and it calmed him. The interview went swimmingly, and he was hired for the position immediately - a wave of relief washed over him. Finally, he could put his financial worries aside.

In the summer of 2004, his employer called him into his office for a meeting. His employer told him that he would be heading off for further training and that it was mandatory. Shahram, excited at the prospect of travel, graciously accepted but he had no idea of what was to come. By September, Shahram was standing on the third story viewing deck of the Eiffel tower and looking out over the city when the warmth of the sun touched his skin. He could barely believe the *serendipity of his training course taking place in Paris. He thought back to the day of his cousin's party and remembered the details of the shoe shop fondly. He couldn't believe how far he had come.*

It took only one year for the universe to bring him from a shoe shop in Iran to the Eiffel Tower in France. Nothing is ever really impossible when we set our imagination into motion and when we are able to define what a vision means to us.

◆ ◆ ◆

This brings us to the end of the Imagination Stage and moves us forward to the third stage in hyper-goal setting for lifelong success – Pray. We have dealt with the systematic functions of hyper-goal setting as well as the psychological ones to some degree, but it is time to get into the deeper work of creating lifelong success. Before you decide to get started on this stage, I want to make some things clear. For some of you the notion of prayer may be something that you feel comfortable with, while for others it may very well be a sensitive subject. If this is a sensitive subject for you, and you are just about getting ready to tune out – wait.

The Prayer Stage is not my attempt to peddle religious facts to anyone; it is my understanding of what a higher power can do for you. As unorthodox as it may seem, prayer does not have to involve God, or any Deity, in the traditional sense. It should only involve your willingness to open yourself up to the possibility of self-fulfillment through the conscious actions. These actions are ignited by putting your dreams out into the universe – or into the realm of a higher power. The notion of a higher power being in play is practically universal. The only thing that changes from person to person is the idea of how that higher power is represented. For some this higher power may be God, or Allah, or Krishna - for some this higher power may be a higher form of self - while for others this higher power may be seen as the thread that ties all of the universe and its energy together. We all have either a voice or sense of intuition that is set off when we face moments of extreme difficulty. This is the higher power that I am going to need you to tap into before moving forward.

In Chapter Three you will come to see just how important the process of finding your inner voice was, and you will be able to identify the moments in which you need to be engaging in prayer. The ways in which you engage with your mind wields an immense amount of power which can set into motion that which you hope to achieve - and this is a point that I will continue to reiterate as we move along. Stay with me for this next chapter, I have a feeling that it will surprise you in the most positive way.

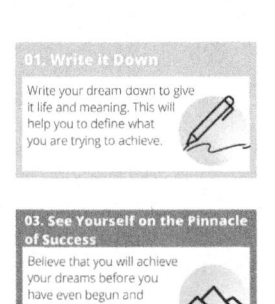

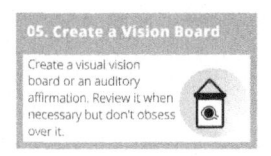

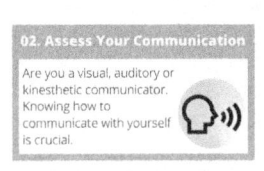

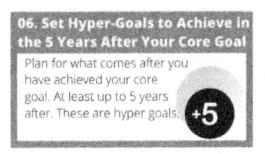

The Imagination Stage: Defining Your Vision

Recap the steps you need to take in order to define your vision during the imagination stage.

01. Write it Down
Write your dream down to give it life and meaning. This will help you to define what you are trying to achieve.

02. Assess Your Communication
Are you a visual, auditory or kinesthetic communicator. Knowing how to communicate with yourself is crucial.

03. See Yourself on the Pinnacle of Success
Believe that you will achieve your dreams before you have even begun and envision it.

04. Be Self-Motivated
Base your goals around your values and your intrinsic motivation will see you through.

05. Create a Vision Board
Create a visual vision board or an auditory affirmation. Review it when necessary but don't obsess over it.

06. Set Hyper-Goals to Achieve in the 5 Years After Your Core Goal
Plan for what comes after you have achieved your core goal. At least up to 5 years after. These are hyper goals.

PRAY

Asking a higher power

Do you believe in the power of prayer? I'm not just speaking about prayer in the traditional sense of the word; I'm speaking about any form of higher conscious speaking. You now know that putting your dreams out into the universe can have a profound effect on whether or not your dreams come true. This is a combination of the use of your capability to wish and the use of your inner voice. In the Prayer Stage of hyper-goal setting, we are going to dive a little deeper into what prayer means to you and how you can harness your higher power to achieve your goals.

I'm often met with concerned looks whenever I speak about prayer. These looks are understandable. In today's world, prayer has a vast array of meanings to different people, and for some this can even be a bit of a sensitive subject. You are reading this right now, which means that you are not afraid to do the necessary and somewhat difficult work of digging a little deeper in order to achieve lifelong success. I didn't promise that it would be easy – there will be moments that may make you uncomfortable and bring you to face-to-face with your true inner identity – but it will be worth it.

We live in a world in which society has a tendency to be more scientific, experimental and materialistic rather than supernatural, spiritual or metaphysical. This is not at all a bad thing, and this is the reason why I offer scientific approaches for some of you who may still be skeptical in terms of spirituality. However, it must be noted that moving away from spirituality can hinder us more than it can help us. There are still many concepts that science does not have the tools to experiment on – or to explain. For thousands of years people have used varying ways of connecting to a higher power – whether it was the use of symbols for protection; worshipping deities; or meditation. Prayer has been catapulted into the full view of the world by religion. Whichever way you see it, religion does not have to be involved in the way which you commit to prayer. Prayer and religion do not have to be inextricably linked. You can decide how you want to engage with your higher power. You can decide who or what you perceive a higher power to be. Let's dive in.

◆ ◆ ◆

The concept of a higher power being at the helm of our lives is not a new concept. It has, however, taken shape and taken on new meaning in recent years. I'm not here to argue whether you should be religious or whether you should believe in God, Allah, Krishna, or any other known Deity – I'm here to guide you on your journey to lifelong success. A tried and tested method that has worked for me time and again involves connecting with a higher power. To you this could be an almighty Deity, it could be the cosmos, it could be the universe, or even just a higher form of your own subconscious. Remember, I am not here to judge or to argue semantics; I am here to set you on the path to achieving your goals. I am merely a catalyst for the changes which you will have to make, and for the actions which you will have to take. At the end of the Prayer Stage of hypergoal setting - if anything - you should have strengthened your inner voice to project your dreams from the Dreaming Stage into a stage of actualization. Your focus should be on positivity

– both putting it out and receiving it.

For some of you, your higher power may be linked to your sixth sense. Dr. Eric Haseltine writes; "If you were sitting in a noisy restaurant with your eyes closed and someone walked by you, say, close to your left side, you'd sense their presence - even if they made no sound. This awareness comes automatically, without you needing to think, 'Hmm. The restaurant noise in my left ear just got more quiet than the noise in my right ear, therefore a sound shadow must have passed by my left side and the most likely source of such a moving shadow would be a walking human.'" (28) This is your body's sixth sense. Your intuition and your collective knowledge of your own existence in relation to the world around you is the epitome of this sixth sense. I have already told you about how immersion in situations and information that support your dream will help you to achieve your dreams. This is one of the exact reasons why. Your sixth sense is honed in your youth, but it can be continually melded by immersing yourself in the information and environments which are needed in order to create the life that you want for yourself. Tapping into your sixth sense could very well be your way of seeking help from a higher power. Your sixth sense is your higher level of consciousness or mental self-awareness.

Whether you believe in prayer, positive self-talk within yourself towards the universe, or aligning your higher consciousness; we will refer to all of these as prayer. When you engage in prayer you are actively engaging with your higher power. Guillermo Vidal refers to this occurrence as "Being in the Flow". When it comes to being in the flow, Vidal says, "I know I have tapped into that Higher Source. This higher power speaks to me through the language of metaphors. It engages my imagination with pictures and visions that speak in ways that are not restricted by mere words. Sometimes, despite my limited vocabulary, I am given words I have never used that better explain (I look up the meaning first, of course) the inspired message."(29) When you actively seek and engage with your higher power, you are able to manifest your dreams and aspirations. You are able to receive the words needed to communicate your vision in a moment of profound clarity.

So how does engaging with your higher power help you to manifest your dreams? It comes down to the strength of your inner voice and your intrinsic motivators. When you utilize them both to communicate internally on a higher plane, you not only condition your own mind to believe that you will succeed; you are also creating a mirror within the universe to see that which you seek. Have you ever been driving and thinking of a yellow car and all of a sudden you see one drive past you? That is because when you focus your mind on something specific you are tuning your mind to look out for it. By engaging your higher power through prayer, you are conditioning your mind to see the signs and be open to them in terms of what you are asking your higher power for. You are aligning yourself with the universe and manifesting the possibility to achieve what you are focusing on during prayer.

Entheo Nation has an interesting theory about being in alignment and it goes like this, "[It's] easy to forget that we are part of the living planet, connected to the web of life, and completely whole and perfect exactly the way we are [...] When you are in a disconnected state, it's hard to know what your purpose is, let alone how to fulfill it. Even if you know what your purpose is, if you are out of alignment, life feels overwhelming and getting things done can be frustrating." (30) So what does this mean? It simply means that if you can tap into your higher power and engage with it, you will be able to pull yourself out of the confusion which this fast-paced world brings you. Once you are able to do that, you will be aligning yourself with a higher purpose that is effectively compounded by your dreams and your intrinsic motivators towards those dreams. It all comes back to being in the flow and going back to the belief that you are purposefully made – you are part of this intricate web of life and you matter.

Many people find that meditating on their dreams or

goals helps them to manifest these goals. This in itself is a form of prayer. Being able to retreat to a quiet place – or a place of inner stillness – allows you to further visualize your success and align your mind and soul in the path of achieving this success. Living in a state of clarity and belief will guide you along your journey.

I will say this again, as it is very important – however you view prayer and whatever your understanding of what a higher power is – you can use this method of positive internal talk to manifest your dreams.

◆ ◆ ◆

So what does asking a higher power do for your balloon?

I want you to think of prayer as helium. As children, not many of us knew the scientific explanation behind why some balloons float and why others don't. A floating balloon seen for the first time is exciting and mystical to a child. The child-like belief that some form of magic exists in the world is what ignites many a dream and breathes life into that dream. A dream that is driven by your higher power is like a balloon which has been filled with helium; while a dream that is not clearly defined and aligned in the universe is a balloon which is filled with regular air. The alignment which you undergo in this stage of hyper-goal setting is the helium that will fill your balloon and allow it to take flight. Just as you should not be afraid to embrace this child-like belief in order to make a wish, you too should not be afraid to embrace your higher power in order to pray.

Prayer is also a very cathartic action. It can wash away the deepest of internal discomforts and put your heart at ease as you navigate difficult situations and decisions on the path to success. It will ultimately help you to manage your emotions and maintain a steady mental balance with your goals. It is the protection you will have against people who could potentially burst your balloon with their opinions. Once you are spiritually centered, you will have an almost unshakeable will. Having faith in something that supports your dreams also creates the will-power needed to achieve your dreams. Whether it is faith in a higher power, or a faith in your own higher consciousness, it can see you through to the pinnacle of success. Remez Sasson for Success Consciousness writes, "Faith, feelings, desire and positive thinking are essential for achieving success, but so [is] positive action, persistence, willpower and self-discipline."[31] A positive mindset and the actions which follow is what prayer is all about. It is about believing in the notion that everything you ask for will be received in one form or another and then trusting in the process enough to let go in order for it to happen organically. Your persistence and self-discipline in terms of staying true to your vision will be the outcome of constant positive self-talk – or prayer.

I want you to think of prayer this way. Each one of us has a certain capacity that we hold within ourselves. Our capacity determines the volume – or the magnitude – of what we can receive.

How so?

Allow me to elaborate. Let's say for instance you have a container with a capacity of 4 liters – just over a gallon. You know that you cannot fit 8 liters – or 2 gallons – into that container. It is literally impossible. You will need a container with a larger volume capacity in order to carry the 8 liters of water that you want.

Similarly, let's say you're driving along and your tire bursts. You are not going to just jump out of your car and lift it off the ground to change your tire. Unless you're the world's strongest man, you don't have the capacity to do that. You just don't have the strength on your own. So what do you do? You use a car jack to lift your car up. This allows you to change your tire without the weight of the car pressing down on you.

Prayer works like a car-jack. It gives you the leverage to get things done that you perhaps wouldn't be able to accomplish on your own. It lifts the weight off of you so that you can focus on what you are doing, and it actually helps you in what you are doing. Prayer is like a supernatural hack to increase your capacity for achievement; it gives you the extra boost – or extra strength – which you need to fulfill your goal.

Let's circle back to your inner capacity. Your mind and soul form your inner container. If your mind and soul don't have the capacity to receive what you are trying to achieve, you are not going to be able to achieve it.

It's that simple.

Prayer increases your spiritual capacity – your capacity to receive. Prayer not only fills your balloon up to its capacity, it increases its capacity. It stretches it and increases the volume which your balloon is able to withhold. If your desire is to own a 1,500 square foot vacation home, you need to stretch your capacity to receive this. If your container – or your cup – cannot hold what you are trying to take hold of, it is just not going to happen. You have to stretch your arms as wide as you can and embrace your dream. Accept it and welcome it in. Generate a spiritual plane which has enough room to cater for your big and boundless dream.

If you think of the universe as if it were the ocean, prayer connects you to your higher power in the same fashion that a drop of water is connected to the ocean. Once you return yourself as a droplet to the ocean, you become one with the ocean. Similarly, when you connect yourself to your higher power, you are becoming one with your higher power. When you engage in prayer, you are removing the limits around your soul. You are allowing your cup to take on much more than it could before. You are realizing your connectedness to the universe and accepting that you are everything and everything is in you. You are going to learn a bit more about this connectedness in the following chapter – Let it Go. There is a spiritual thread that connects everyone and everything in the universe. When you engage your higher power, you move in unison with this thread; you reveal your purpose to yourself; and you open yourself up for success.

Once you are able to increase your capacity through prayer, you will be able to accommodate new things which you have never been able to before. Whatever your heart desires; and whatever you are able to communicate, as well as wish for, will come to be through the power of prayer. Prayer also gives you a priceless lever to pivot all of your potential. Once you are of the mindset that this very simple – yet powerful – tool can actually help you to achieve all things, it gives you the confidence to think big and act in big ways. Your confidence and belief in your capacity will see you through. Now, it must be said that there are other parts of your life that will help you to increase your capacity. However, you are not always in control of these things – as with most things in life. Things such as the hardships you go through in life lead to growth and increase the capacity of your cup. Prayer, however, is the one technique that allows you to increase your capacity in a positive way – without the necessity for hardship.

I have already expressed how everything that is, was, or ever will be has already been created. Energy cannot be created or destroyed – only harnessed. Prayer allows you the capacity to receive that which is meant for you. It is already there, you just have to harness – or manifest it.

◆ ◆ ◆

A question I am often asked: "is there a right moment for prayer?" There is no such thing as a right moment for prayer, but if you would like, you can set aside a specific time to engage in your own form of prayer. Whether this is getting on your knees and talking to God or it is sitting silently with your legs crossed while meditating into a realm of higher consciousness - how you pray is inconsequential. The only thing that should be of relevance to you is what you derive from prayer when you engage in it. So let us circle back again.

Is there a right time for prayer?

No there is not.

Anytime is the right time for prayer. You don't have to set aside a specific time, but you can if routine and structure help you. As this stage is a very personal journey, how and when you choose to engage in prayer will be relative to you, your beliefs and your desires.

One thing that I can suggest for you is the use of positive affirmation through prayer. So what is positive affirmation? Positive affirmation is the process of speaking with gratitude for what you are yet to receive. It is a great way - for anyone who is not inclined to use prayer in the traditional sense of the word - to still harness the positive impact of prayer. Let's look at how you can speak with gratitude over something you are yet to receive. Take a moment of meditation for example; using a mantra during meditation has proven to have an incredibly calming effect. Many of us are incapable of clearing our minds for long enough to hold a blank mental image over a prolonged period. Since you are required to clear your mind during meditation, this can prove to be a bit difficult. Now, it is good to note that the practice of clearing your mind has been broadened over the years. When you are told to clear your mind as an instruction for meditation, you are not being told to stop thinking altogether; that is virtually impossible. Instead you should find something that you can focus on in order to clear your mind of everything else. So how do you utilize this in combination with positive affirmation to create your own method of 'prayer'?

Allow me to explain.

If you choose to meditate for a period of your day, I want you to focus on a positive statement – an expression of gratitude. Let's use wanting to own a school as an example again. Your positive affirmation would go a little something like this; "I am grateful for the path that I am on. I am grateful for where I am, and I am grateful for the school that I am about to receive." A short and simple mantra of gratitude that you can use in order to focus your mind, relax your body and engage in positive self-talk. This method of positive affirmation and expressing gratitude is widely accepted across all beliefs. Marketing Mentor,

John Eggen advises on just how to engage in prayer whether or not you are religious:
1. "Acknowledge and call-upon your Higher Power, however you conceive of it, and whatever you call it."
2. "Ask your Higher Power for whatever you want regarding your [goal], and by when. Use whatever language to do it that's natural for you."
3. "Express gratitude to your Higher Power for hearing your prayer, and for responding to it."
4. "Repeat the above 3 steps daily with genuine devotion and gratitude." (32)

This is a simple and effective way to speak using positive affirmation, and to use gratitude as your point of departure in order to manifest exactly what you want in terms of your goal. You are also allowing yourself to have a moment of clarity that is just between you and your higher power which will allow you to put a verbal meaning to your goal – whether this is done orally or mentally is entirely up to you. Engaging in prayer using this method gives you a daily motivational pep-talk, of sorts. As time passes, the more that you are able to connect with your higher power, the more clarity you will be able to achieve. I have even had great success in forming new ideas as well as refining my ideas during – and immediately after – prayer. This is not just due to what I believe to be divine - or cosmic - intervention, but due to the fact that I am fully immersed in a moment that is solely focused on my purpose, my higher power and my goal. If you are skeptical on the amazing effects that prayer can have on your life, I ask only that you give it a chance and allow it take on meaning in your life. I can assure you that as time goes on it will be a highly important part of your daily ritual where you will obtain a wealth of self-awareness and knowledge.

The 7 Habits of Highly Effective People late author, Stephen Covey once said that his morning routine included prayer, and he said, "I go into my library and pray with a listening spirit, listening primarily to my conscience while I visualize the rest of my entire day, including important professional activities and key relationships with my loved ones, working associates and clients. I see myself living by correct principles and accomplishing worthy purposes." (33) His process of prayer included the use of positive affirmation. He could visualize himself accomplishing those worthy purposes, and living by correct principles. He put out into the universe that which he hoped to be for the day, and that which he hoped to achieve. He then set about believing wholeheartedly in that image before it came to be. Throughout the entirety of your goal-setting journey towards success, visualization will come up time and time again. This is because the likelihood of your success will depend on your mental capacity to visualize, and then to act on those visualizations. Prayer is the deepest form of this visualization technique. You may very well believe in listening to your conscience as Stephen Covey did. This, as I mentioned, is a form of your higher-self and this could be your own higher power. By living a life that is aligned with your core values, listening to your conscience and engaging with this inner voice, you are engaging in a form of prayer. All you have to do is acknowledge it at a deeper level and go about your prayer in a way that has a conscious and real impact on you.

If meditation and traditional prayer are not something that you can foresee yourself engaging in, there are alternatives here too. Remember, my understanding of prayer is anything that opens you up to positive self-talk which you put out towards a higher power – or the universe. You may very well be a spiritual person without being aware of it. That morning run that you take to clear your mind before you start your day - or retreating to the mountains for a weekend of hiking - are forms of reaching out to your higher self. Prayer involves doing away with the noise of the outside world and speaking either out loud, or within your own mind, in a way which allows for the truest and most vulnerable form of your inner self to take center stage. It is a process of de-cluttering the information of the day, switching off and returning your mind to a clean starting point from which you can focus on your innermost desires in a positive and calm manner. There is an old Cherokee tale that involves an old man and his grandson, which goes somewhat along these lines: *"My son, there is a battle between two wolves inside us all.*

One is Evil. It is anger, jealousy, greed, resentment, inferiority, lies, and ego. The other is Good. It is joy, peace, love, hope, humility, kindness, empathy, and truth." The boy thought about it, and asked, *"Grandfather, which wolf wins?"* The old man quietly replied, *"The one you feed."*

Prayer allows you to feed the good wolf. Prayer allows you to seek your higher power from a place of humility; as well as to speak your truth over that which you love and are passionate about. Prayer fills you with hope and brings you joy. Your higher-power in essence, is your good wolf.

Your subconscious already contains almost all of the elements needed for you to succeed. You wouldn't have a dream within you that you could not achieve. As long as you are in energetic alignment with your goals, and those goals are in alignment with your core values, you have already laid most of the groundwork for your path to success. Emma Bathie for Goalcast, mentions that people who are in energetic alignment with their goals "bring their dreams to life by simply focusing on the joy it brings them and others, and they can't imagine their life any other way [...] They take time each day to give thanks, and to enjoy some sort of spiritual practice such as meditation, time out in nature or a combination of the two."[34] You can pick up almost any other goal-setting book, tap into any goal-setting blog, and I assure you spiritual awareness and some form of prayer will be mentioned. Although I may use a new method of goal-setting, there are still some tried and tested 'helpers' along the way that can aid you in achieving the success you so desire. I need you to trust me when I say that prayer is one of these tried and tested helpers. People who go on to achieve lifelong success through their goals have an unwavering belief in their higher power and in the fact that their higher power – or the universe – is on their team. They genuinely believe that anything that they ask of their higher power will come to be, and that it is just a matter of time. They envision what they desire and they repeat a mantra, or a prayer, or a positive affirmation; and breathe life into it. If you can tap into this faith and this belief in your higher power – whatever that may be to you – I have no doubt in my mind that you will have greatly increased your odds for success.

◆ ◆ ◆

Prayer can be just as important in all aspects of your life and has been proven to greatly improve one's overall wellbeing and health. Whether you believe that it is a higher power divinely intervening in your life, or that it is the power of your own mind; prayer can have great benefits for your life. I have a feeling that some of you might still be skeptical, so let's take a scientific approach to this for a moment. Have you ever believed so deeply in a possible outcome that it manifested itself right before your eyes? Prayer can have the same effect on your life.

It all comes down to belief.

Many studies have been conducted on the power of the placebo effect. Now, at the risk of calling your higher power a placebo, please know that this is not my intention at all. I offer no offenses in what I am about to tell you. I simply want to offer a scientific approach to prayer for those of you that may be skeptical, so please read on. The psychological phenomena known as the placebo effect occurs when a patient is given a null-treatment such as a sugar-pill for a specific illness. Due to the patient's belief that the pill which they have been given will actually treat them, their mind triggers a phenomenon whereby the patient experiences significant positive results from that sugar-pill. Kendra Cherry for Very Well Mind writes; "The expectations of the patient can play a significant role in the placebo effect. The more a person expects the treatment to work, the more likely they are to exhibit a placebo response." (35)

So what does this mean for you in terms of prayer?

I believe it simply means that if you believe strongly enough that your higher power will answer your prayers, it will come to be. Whether you are praying over good health, marital success, or the success of your goals – prayer can have an incredibly powerful effect on your life just because you believe in its power. Similarly, your lack of belief in what you are asking for - and from whom you are asking it – can have a negative impact on the fulfillment of your goals.

In the following chapter, Let It Go, you will come to see that once you have put something out into the universe, you need to let it go. I'll touch on this very briefly here because we will look at this in greater detail in the chapter to follow. The basis of letting go is as such; once you have sent your prayer out for the day – if you are engaging daily, which I highly recommend you do – let it go. Don't let the words that you used, or whether or not you were specific enough consume you. Your higher power is not a genie; you are not going to be tricked into something not meant for you because you didn't mentally word it correctly. Your higher power - whether God, the universe, or your higher self – knows your heart. Don't focus on wording, don't focus on the specifics of how you've submitted your request, focus on opening up your true self and then let it go for the day. Simply open up your method of communication and tap into your receptive communication type. Prayer should be there to guide you; to clarify your purpose; and to allow you a moment to relieve yourself of your thoughts, but it should not overwhelm you.

Prayer can also have other benefits on your life. As you begin praying for what it is you wish to accomplish, you begin to feel as though you can communicate your innermost ideas better. A routine theme of positive self-talk in the form of prayer allows your mind to use a higher form of communication. It unlocks parts of yourself that you had previously tucked away and allows your most authentic voice to take center stage.

Have you ever had an oral exam or had to make a presentation at work?

You practiced your talking points long before going in for either of these, didn't you? Prayer allows you this moment of practice. By repeating what you want on a continual basis, you are practicing communicating what it is that you want, enabling yourself to address your goal very briefly but meaningfully. This gives you a better understanding of your goal itself and may even lead to breakthroughs in terms of how you wish to change to become in energetic alignment with that goal.

Prayer further allows your mind, body and spirit to be in complete unison. I have already discussed the potentially positive effects that meditation can have on your life, as well as on the outcome of your goals. Prayer can also allow you to transcend the noise of the day in the same way that meditation can. It is a quiet and reflective act of self-love. It is a moment that is totally for you. While it is important to live a life in service of others, as you will come to see in Chapter Five, you need to be pouring from a full cup. This means that you need to be nurturing yourself before you can commit to serving others. In balancing the "car" that is your life you can sometimes fall out of that balance as you attempt to maintain relationships with colleagues, friends and family. Prayer allows you to center yourself, and focus wholly on yourself without the expectations of the outside world interfering with your train of thought. In a fast paced world it is also easy to become out of touch with your body. The stress of this fast pace can have detrimental effects on your health, and we'll discuss this further in Let It Go.

When you engage in a moment of solitude and center your mind before moving on to your prayer, your heart rate and your movements are slow enough for you to pick up on certain stressors that you may have been missing during the course of a busy day. Remember that this entire process needs to work for you - and with you - as you begin to move into a flowing and rhythmic, growth-mindset. At the core of all of this work, if you are not centered in the pursuit of your goals, you are going to burn out before you have even had the chance to taste the fruits of your labor. Allow yourself the time to immerse in connecting with your higher power and you will have unlocked a doorway to serenity amidst an ever-changing and chaotic world. Another significant point to be aware of is that trauma can creep up on you when you least expect it. Many people often find themselves revisiting past traumas in the form of flashbacks once they have achieved that which they have set out to. This is due to the fact that trauma is an after effect of a traumatic experience. You could go through some of the most harrowing experiences and walk away feeling unscathed only to find yourself reeling from the shock years after the experience.

It's like whiplash.

You walk away from an accident feeling perfectly fine, and when you wake up the next day you are riddled with aches and pains. When you are traumatized by something you may only start seeing the effects of this trauma as things start to go well for you. People have been known to get anxious at specific times of day because that is when they experienced the trauma. Prayer allows you to navigate these moments as they happen. It works to lighten the load which you are bearing so that when you do begin to achieve success, you are not flooded with a wave of memories and negative emotions. When you begin to achieve that which your heart desires, it is like your body goes into a shift, and you may feel less anxious about the goal itself as it starts to come to fruition. If you are not spiritually prepared, your adrenal relaxation could open the emotional flood gates of past stressors and trauma.

As I mentioned earlier, prayer allows you to transcend the noise of the outside world and once you are in a meditative-like state, not only are you slowing your heart rate but also slowing your breathing. Your body goes into a relaxed state that has been proven to even help in the reduction of blood-pressure. This could also be largely due to the fact that engaging in prayer has been known to reduce anger and aggression. A 2011 study revealed that after "a series of experiments in which participants either prayed for or thought about a stranger, a person who angered them or a friend in need, members of the prayer group were more likely to feel less anger and aggression after a provocation."[36] Kristen Rogers, for CNN, recently wrote about the scientific and psychological benefits of the mind-soul connection through prayer. In her article she elaborated on the ability of prayer to reduce anger, and also on the ability for prayer to see people over immensely difficult hurdles in life. That being said, scientific experiments such as these do not attempt to verify or discredit the existence of a higher power, but rather to reveal the power of belief. It is all tied together – belief in yourself; belief in your vision; and belief in your higher power. Rogers also goes on to reference Dr. Christina Puchalski, a professor of medicine and health science at George Washington University, whom has said "[People] pray for specific outcomes; to share their angst and suffering in a relational context; to show gratitude; and to reflect." [37]

Reflect.

Prayer is not something you should only be turning to in moments of need or fear, it is something you should be turning to prevent moments of fear. It is something you should be turning to in order to reflect on your life, your goals and your difficulties. Mirror, or reflect, that which is going on around you in order to understand it better. Become the mirror yourself and reflect that which you wish to receive in order to clarify it – and then reach out and grab it.

◆ ◆ ◆

Let's recap the Prayer Stage of hyper-goal setting before moving on to Chapter Four.
When I speak about prayer, I'm not just speaking about it in the traditional sense of the word; I'm speaking about any form of higher conscious speaking. Putting your dreams out into the universe can have a profound effect on whether or not your dreams come true. This is a combination of the use of your

capability to wish and the use of your inner voice. You may now be more aware of what prayer means to you and how you can harness this higher power to achieve your goals. Know this: prayer and religion do not have to be inextricably linked. However, we must note that our societal shift from a spiritual way of engaging with the world around us to a more scientific way can do us more harm than good. There are still many concepts that science does not have the tools to explain.

The concept of a higher power being at the helm of our lives is not a new concept. It has, however, taken shape and taken on new meaning in recent years. I'm not here to argue whether you should be religious, or whether you should believe in God, Allah, Krishna, or any other known Deity. I'm here to guide you on your journey to lifelong success, and a tried and tested method that has worked for me time and time again involves connecting with a higher power. To you this could be an almighty Deity, it could be the cosmos, it could be the universe, or even just a higher form of your own subconscious. Remember, I am not here to judge or to argue semantics; I am here to set you on the path to achieving your goals. I am merely a catalyst for the actions which you will have to take.

I want you to think of prayer as helium in terms of your balloon. As children, not many of us knew the scientific explanation behind why some balloons float and why others don't. A floating balloon seen for the first time is exciting and mystical to a child. The child-like belief that some form of magic exists in the world is what ignites many a dream and breathes life into that dream. A dream that is driven by your higher power is like a balloon which has been filled with helium. Furthermore, each one of us has a certain capacity that we hold within ourselves. Our capacity determines the volume of what we can receive. Remember the example of a container with a capacity of 4 liters. You will need a container with a larger volume capacity to carry the 8 liters of water. Prayer increases your inner capacity and it is like the lever which you can use to pivot all of your inner potential.

There is no such thing as a right moment for prayer, but if you would like, you can set aside a specific time to engage in your own form of prayer. I highly recommend engaging in prayer on a daily – or regular – basis. Whether this is getting on your knees and talking to God or it is sitting silently with your legs crossed while meditating into a realm of higher consciousness, how you pray is inconsequential. The only thing that should be of relevance to you is what you derive from prayer when you engage in it. Anytime is the right time for prayer. You don't have to set aside a specific time, but you can if you want to. One thing which I suggest is the use of positive affirmation through prayer. Speak with gratitude for what you are yet to receive. It is a great way for anyone who is not inclined to use prayer in the traditional sense of the word to still harness the positive impact that traditional prayer has.

Prayer can be just as important in all aspects of your life and has been proven to greatly improve one's overall wellbeing and health. Whether you believe that it is a higher power divinely intervening in your life, or that it is the power of your own mind, it can have great benefits for your life. Many scientific studies have been conducted on the power of a psychological phenomenon known as the placebo effect. It simply highlights that if you believe strongly enough in the power of something, your belief can make it come to be. Whether you are praying over good health, marital success, or the success of your goals – prayer can have an incredibly powerful effect on your life just because you believe in its power. Similarly, your lack of belief in what you are asking for can have a negative impact on the fulfillment of your goals. Prayer is not something you should only be turning to in moments of need or fear, it is something you should be turning to prevent moments of fear. It is something you should be turning to in order to reflect on your life, your goals and your difficulties. Mirror or reflect that which is going on around you in order to understand it better. Become the mirror yourself and reflect that which you wish to receive in order to clarify it.

Anything that you put out into the universe in genuine and heartfelt prayer will come to be, and I am living proof of this. Allow me to tell you a story about just how prayer changed my life.

◆ ◆ ◆

In the year 2009, I had been experiencing high levels of stress due to work pressure as well as my own family issues. I ended up quitting my job that same year and I was faced with the task of finding an alternative source of income. I had a decent amount set away in my savings and I decided that I would learn how to day trade on the stock market. I would use my savings as my start-up capital, and I was sure that it would work itself out. At the very same time, I had listed my apartment in my hometown of Isfahan for sale. The buyer seemed honest and capable so we agreed on a payment plan of sorts. He would pay me off in three instalments.

The problem therein was that I had already made an offer on an apartment in the Iranian capital; Tehran. I had written a post-dated cheque for the apartment which I had offered to purchase. The cheque was set to clear in just three days, but the man who had signed to purchase my apartment was only to commence payments the following month. I had lost almost all of my savings on the stock market and there was nothing in my bank account to go towards the cheque for the apartment in Tehran. I was in an incredibly difficult financial situation, and it only seemed to be getting worse. You see, at the time I was living in an employee property that belonged to the company from which I had just resigned. I was given a week to vacate the premises. So there I was; no job, no source of income, no savings, a huge amount set to go off my empty bank account, and no sight of even the first payment on the apartment that I had sold. A bounced cheque would have been enough to ruin my financial credit, and years of discipline in terms of my finances. Not only this, but the circumstances surrounding the amount, the offer to purchase and the backlash of an empty bank account, could have been a legally punishable offence. I wish I could convey to you just how distraught I felt at that mo-

ment. I can remember it as if it were yesterday. It felt like the whole world was crashing down around me as I stared out at the sunset on that gloomy Tuesday evening. I can remember how my body began to shake from sheer nervousness and anxiety around the situation.

Almost as if a little voice went off in my head, I heard what seemed like a whisper – it told me to reach out to God. I sat down and I began talking to God. I asked him for help with a heaviness in my heart that I had not felt before. I didn't pray in a way that you would traditionally expect.

I spoke.

I spoke to God as if he were a close friend, explaining everything that I had been going through. I laid my forehead against the ground and it was as if someone had opened the floodgates. I began to weep. Just as suddenly as this emotion had rushed through me, it dissipated and I felt incredibly calm and comforted. I was no longer cold. The shaking and shivering had ceased; and I felt this warmth, like a small child embraced close to their mother's bosom.

I lingered in that overwhelming moment before standing up; and when I did I felt empowered. I wiped my tears and smiled as I heard the voice whisper again – it then told me that everything was going to be ok. Just a few hours later, my phone rang and I was shocked to see who was calling. An old friend of mine was on the other end. We talked for a while and caught up before he said that he had wanted to check up on me – he asked me if everything was ok. With a sigh, I told him that I was not alright. I began explaining my living situation; elaborating that I had a cheque of 60 million Tomans - approximately US$60,000 at the time – set to go off of my account and that I had almost no money in that very account. He paused for a moment and expressed his sympathy for my situation. He assured me that everything would find a way to work itself out. After a few exchanges, we bid each other farewell; promising not to stay out of touch for so long this time.

I woke up the next morning feeling a little disappointed, but nonetheless motivated that I would find a way to rectify what had transpired. I would find a way to get back on track financially. I had prayed over it, and there was literally very little that I could at that point. Rather than worry about it, I put it to God and tried to let it go. I had just made myself a cup of coffee when I received a banking in-contact text reflecting an incoming transfer of 61 million Tomans. If my jaw was not attached to my face, it would have dropped right down to the floor in that moment. I was in shock; where had this money come from? I recalled the conversation with my old friend and I cupped my face; smiling and giggling like a young boy. I just couldn't believe it. My friend later explained to me that he had sent me 60 million Tomans for the cheque towards my new apartment in Tehran, and a further 1 million Tomans towards my living expenses over the next month – just until I could get the first payment in for the apartment which I had sold.

A moment that had the potential to ruin my life, my finances, and my good standing with the law, had turned itself around. I hadn't gone out seeking help from anyone other than my higher power, and I was provided everything that I needed. It may not have happened in the way that I had planned, but my faith allowed it to happen nonetheless. Even in your darkest moments, always have faith that what is meant for you will come to be and that everything in life has a way of working itself out.

◆ ◆ ◆

Now that we have reached the end of the prayer stage of hyper-goal setting, you are going to be moving on to a technique which is going to set you free of expectation and worry. In the chapter to follow - Let it Go - you will come to see the importance of being in the flow which I have spoken of in this chapter. Being in the flow means accepting that which you cannot control and moving with the changes which will ultimately occur along your journey to success. To reach your target, you will have to look away from it momentarily to focus on what is right in front of you. This may come as a shock to you as you have spent the last few chapters locking into your target as well as envisioning and defining it – you have even begun to pray over it. However, once you have all of this in place, you must let it go. You cannot breathe life into something by holding on to it so tightly that you begin to choke the life out of it. We have a bit more work to do, so let's get started

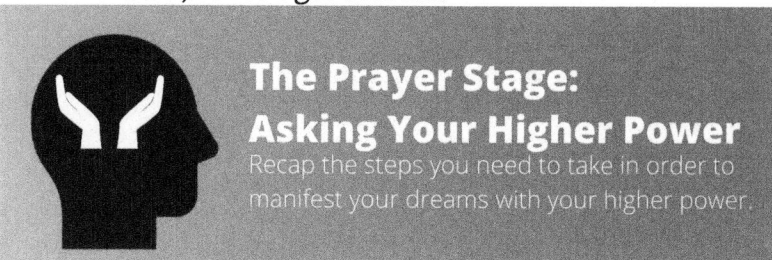

The Prayer Stage: Asking Your Higher Power

Recap the steps you need to take in order to manifest your dreams with your higher power.

01. Prayer & Religion are not Exclusive

Religion and prayer do not have to be inextricably linked. Even if you are not religious, you can still engage in prayer. It's all about spirituality.

02. What Higher Power Means to You

You may feel that your higher power is an almighty deity, the universe, or even your own higher self. Whatever you believe it to be, tap into it.

03. Prayer is Like Helium

Prayer fills your balloon up and allows it to take flight. Not only does it fill it up to capacity, it stretches it and increases its capacity.

04. No "Right Time" for Prayer

Anytime is a good time for prayer. I would, however, highly suggest making it a part of your daily routine and affirmations.

05. Prayer for Your Wellbeing

Prayer can have incredibly calming effects. It is also known to reduce aggression, and high blood pressure.

LET IT GO

Setting your mind free

You have dreamt of your goals, you have defined them in greater detail and you have even prayed on it. The next stop on your hyper-goal setting journey for lifelong success is to let your dream go. I know that this may seem counterproductive, but it is the exact opposite. You have done most of the work that needs to be done in moving towards achieving your goals. If you hold on to your goals too tightly you can become consumed by them. Maintaining focus and motivation is not the same as being obsessed about something. Being obsessed is a sure-fire way to cloud your mind and make rash and impulsive decisions, not only when it comes to your goals, but when it comes to your personal life as well.

I already spoke of the balance which is necessary in order to live a fulfilled and happy life, and you will realize the validity of those points in this stage of hyper-goal setting. When you become consumed by your goals you are messing with the delicate balance of your life. Your physical body, your brain, your soul, your close connections and your finances can all be negatively impacted and thrown out of balance. When you are too intensely focused on your goals, you can lose sight of the imbalance that it is causing, and before you know it, it is too late to repair some of the damage which your obsession has caused.

This form of fixation can lead to severe stress which in turn can lead to poor health. It is no secret that people who do not manage stress of this nature in an effective manner, often end up with psychological breaks as well as physical problems such as heart disease, amongst many others. Competitive runner, Tina Muir, describes her own experience with this phenomenon: "[Sometimes], being more committed isn't the right thing to do. Certainly in the running world, it is a dangerous line to walk, the line between commitment and obsession [...] Time and time again, I have people reach out to me, telling me just how committed they are, just how much time they are putting into the sport [...] Yet they are being punished by the running gods with an injury, burnout, overtraining, bad races. You name it, it happens."(38) You would think that for something as physically attainable as a running goal, the harder you push yourself physically, the better your running times or outcomes would be – but this is not the case. An imbalanced obsession with the sport, just like any other obsession, can lead to detrimental physical and mental damage.

The negative impact that small continual "failures" can have on your motivation is incredibly high. An overstrained body and spirit will never be able to perform at optimum levels. You will be constantly run down, demotivated and emotionally exhausted. It is important to remain focused on your dream but to allow it to manifest itself as a part of your life. Remember, achieving your goal is only a doorway for all that is to come in your journey to lifelong success. Your goal is a part of your journey; it does not encompass the entirety of your journey and should not take up all of your mental, emotional or spiritual space.

Your dreams must be allowed to take flight. The only way that we can fulfill this next step is simply to acknowledge them, but to let them go. You have already breathed life into your balloon. You have given it definition and your prayer has acted as the helium which has stretched it and filled it up. The best thing that a helium-filled balloon does is float, or fly. So let your balloon take flight by letting go of that string. When you hold on to your dream too tightly it is like locking up your opportunities and the universe has no space to run its course in fulfilling your dreams. When you hover over your dream like a helicopter parent over a child, your dream has no space to flourish and take shape in its own way. You cannot be 100% in control all of the time and trying to do so will only cause you an immense amount of stress and lead you to miss out on other opportunities that may arise for you to pursue your dreams. You must be in the flow of things. You must be open to the idea of an ever-evolving dream and an ever-changing environment.

Business coach Jamie Cunningham writes; "Consider when you meet someone but can't remember their name. The harder you focus on it, the more difficult it becomes to bring their name to mind, only to find the moment you move on and focus on something else; it comes back to you [...] Once we release our emotional attachment around something, we make some room for opportunity to come towards us versus thinking that to achieve a specific goal we need to stick to a certain path, and end up developing a resistance to it."(39) Following a path when it comes to achieving your goals is absolutely crucial, but what you need to be open to is the fact that this path may change - or fork - as time progresses. Don't be so intensely focused on the path that you miss out on the opportunities to achieve your dreams down a slightly different looking avenue. Over-exerting yourself will only dry up your motivation and make you frustrated and angry. You may become angry towards the fact that your dream is not manifesting in the way that you would like it to, or that the journey is not turning out the way which you had expected it to. This is another key reason why mid-term goals suck; they set you up for failure by giving you the notion that in order to achieve your goal you must stay the exact course with them. Having shorter-term goals and one long-term goal as well as several post-goals alleviates this problem and makes it easier for you to let go and trust in the process.

There is an immense amount of emotional relief that is derived from letting go. Fixating causes your body to go into stress mode. Ann Pietrangelo and Stephanie Watson write for Healthline; "[If] your stress response doesn't stop firing, and these stress levels stay elevated far longer than is necessary for survival, it can take a toll on your health. Chronic stress can cause a variety of symptoms and affect your overall well-being." (40) Other than irritability and other psychological problems, this stress can manifest itself physically, as I have already briefly mentioned. If you remain in a constant state of stress, you may end up experiencing any of the following symptoms: headaches, insomnia, heightened acid reflux, a weakened immune system, high blood pressure, fertility problems, reduced sex drive and many more. There is nothing on earth that is worth risking your health for. When it comes to chronic illnesses there are many that cannot be easily treated, or fixed. What is the point of having money and success that you can't enjoy because your body is run down and incapable of functioning normally? What is the point in creating the life of your dreams if your stress has decimated relationships with your loved ones? The real key to happiness is a balanced and healthy lifestyle. Your goals can help you to unlock the potential for lifelong success, but if your goals are driving you to ill health – mentally and physically – you need to reassess your method and learn to let go. Let's move on to how you can engage in short-term goal setting to eradicate mid-term goals and alleviate this stress.

◆ ◆ ◆

At this stage you should be working on letting your long-term goal go. This is not to say that you should forget about it. It will always be in the forefront of what you do because you have gone through all the necessary previous steps to cement this. What you should be focusing on at this stage are your short-term goals. These should ideally be achievable within three months. Set out for short-term goals and focus on one at a time. Forget the rest for now.

Your short-term goals should be aligned with your vision, and you will be able to achieve this by revisiting your vision board. We're going to circle back to the school as an example here. Your short-term goals in terms of wanting own a school could include devising a name for the school, compiling research documents in support of your dream, and even registering a business trademark. How you sequence these short term goals could be informed by the legalities surrounding your goal. When it comes to setting short-term goals for a business, it is always wise to set your research documents as your first set of short-term goals. These will inform you on all other short-term goals and, depending on your industry, you may even be lucky enough to be given deadline guidance in the form of application date deadlines for licensing and so on.

So why do I say medium or mid-term goals suck?

Mid-term goals generally run from six months to three years to achieve. How much can change in a year? Setting mid-term goals can add to the stress that I spoke of because as your environment constantly changes, your mid-term goals are likely to be rendered redundant long before you have even gotten close to achieving them. This perceived failure could put a damper on your motivation and lead to a high level of frustration. Put it this way, if your dream is to own a school and you work around mid-term goals, one of those mid-term goals could very well be breaking ground to begin construction. All of your goals that follow will end up hinging on this mid-term goal. Now you will have to break ground eventually, but bringing this to the forefront of your mind and giving it the importance of being a mid-term goal is an unnecessary weight to carry. Your short-term goals and subsequent goals will end up being focused around this instead of being focused around your long-term goal and hyper-goals. Placing that level of importance on breaking ground means that if, for whatever reason, that goal moves further and further away from the deadline you have set for it, you begin to focus on this as a failure when it is not. It is just the path changing, as can be expected along your journey.

So how do you set short-term goals?

A great acronym to use is SMART. Ideapod describes this as making your goals "Specific, Measurable, Attainable, Realistic, [and] Timely." (41) Just as you have set measurable targets for your long-term goal and the hyper-goals to follow, you will have to do the same for your short-term goals. The point of letting go is not to become wishy-washy about when and how you want to achieve certain things, you will still need some sort of structure in place – what you do need to let go of is the incessant need to control all of these minute details, should the path begin to change.

Carpenter for Ideapod goes on to write, "A long-term goal can still be successful, but it's so hard to measure it without the help of short-term goals. The days may be long, but the weeks are short, and before you know it, that five years is up. You look back and think, what have I done with my life?" (42) Your short-term goals will help you achieve your long-term goal and subsequent goals. This is the reason why it was very important for you to have created a clear vision as per your core or long-term goal and the reason why you want to achieve it – in other words the reason for the core goal is what it will do for your life via subsequent hyper-goals.

Short-term goals are incredibly important in keeping you motivated but they also help you to increase your productivity. When a long-term goal is broken down into smaller, easily attainable and actionable steps, checking off each milestone – or short-term goal – along the way will keep you determined and productive. Other than this, short-term goals also help you to eradicate procrastination. I'm sure many of us have seen the meme circulating on social media that says, "The reason why I procrastinate so much is because I still manage to get it done even though I procrastinate."

Funny?

Sure.

However, this fails to acknowledge the fact that procrastination can cause severely high levels of anxiety and stress. Removing the opportunity for procrastination altogether by creating short-term actionable goals, is yet another way to attain lifelong success, and a stress-reduced life, as you pursue your goals.

Now, I need to clarify something – in the process of setting your short-term goals, it is incredibly important to not become enveloped or overwhelmed by them. Remember that the key to achieving your goals in a stress-reduced manner is to not overplan or overthink what you are setting out to do. Your goals are there to motivate you, not to dictate your life. Set your short-term goals one at a time, if you can. Setting goals any further into the future than this constitutes a mid-term goal; and these suck! Try not to forget it.

Let's get back to the school legalities. You will have an estimate of the sequence of events that should go off before you can officially open the school. Things such as business registration, site inspections and so on. You can very well use this as a guide, but don't place a barrier in front of yourself by insisting that they be completed by a specific date. Focus on the sequence, not the deadline.

So how does this work?

Focus on the very first step; let's say for arguments sake that this is business research and registration. Make that your only primary focus. Don't worry about sitting in front of the board of education, don't worry about breaking ground, and don't worry about site inspections. You know that there is a sequence to how these events will take place but don't put a deadline on them. Just focus on registering the business. After you have registered the business, you can focus on the next step and only that next step. Let everything else go. Keep your focus right in front of you. Focus on putting one foot in front of the other – nothing more. In doing this, you are focusing on the wins and not on how near or far you are to accomplishing your core goal. How awesome is it to feel like you are constantly winning? This is exactly what setting and accomplishing short-term goals does for you. It gives you a much needed confidence boost in what is going to be a very long journey. It keeps you fired up and excited about the next step.

Who wants to hold off on a win?

Nobody!

When you can actively see yourself winning continually via these short-term goals, it will also help to keep you afloat during times of difficulty. You will be able to look back on all the seemingly small milestones you have achieved and feel confident to keep going. I want to speak a little more about the importance of not attempting to plan on a year-by-year basis, and the dangers of comparing your timeline to others.

◆ ◆ ◆

You are probably wondering how you are going to accomplish your goal without having mid-term goals or having a plan by year in place. It is quite simple and it will actually work in your favor, because you cannot plan year-by-year up to the point that you reach your ultimate goal - it is far too complicated. When you set a long-term goal, the likelihood is that the goal involves something that you have never achieved before – otherwise you wouldn't be placing this much importance on it. How can you possibly plan every little detail along the way? You can research as much as you would like to, but the path will change along the way, believe me. Your immersive research and surrounding yourself with information in support of your goal is only to motivate you in the fact that it can be done - your goal can be achieved. This immersive technique is only there to help you envision what can be achieved. It is not there to inform you of what each year of the process will look like. Of course, you can look to people whom have achieved what you are setting out to achieve for inspiration, but you cannot compare the timeline of their success to plan your own. Comparisons like this are quite dangerous in the sense that you will be putting extra pressure on yourself to accomplish these year-long, or even three-year-long, mid-term goals in the same timeline and fashion as those mentors whom you are looking towards. You've already seen in Chapter One how two people in a similar situation can have a very different outcome based on the way that they think and engage with their environment. The very same applies here. You cannot possibly adhere to a timeline set out by someone else because you do not live the same lives; you do not walk the same path; and you do not think the same way. Every human mind, albeit powerful, is incredibly unique but one thing that we all tend to lean towards is the incessant need to plan and control everything around us – it is a pre-wired survival instinct.

Remember flight-or-fight mode?

This is it, in its highest form. Fear of the unknown, and the resulting stress reaction, is what drives us to overthink and overanalyze every little aspect of our lives. We become so busy planning that we are no longer living. Surrender to the unknown and embrace the process. Circumnavigate your fight-or-flight responses and be in the flow of things.

Comparing your timeline to those whom have gone before you is a one-way ticket to depression, anxiety and feelings of self-loathing. Don't do this to yourself. Remember that everything that is, ever was, or ever will be has already been created. You do not have to carry the weight of creation on your shoulders. You only have to harness your inner power to step through the doorway of opportunity. One of the key reasons why you shouldn't try to set mid-term targets, or compare your timeline to that of others, is that you would be comparing against a façade. People very rarely show you their true struggles, or every detail of their lives. We are all entitled to some level of privacy, are we not? The chances are that the people whom you will be tempted to compare yourself to have a lot more going on in the background than they let on. Save yourself the heartache and let it go. Look to mentors for inspiration, not for comparison. You may know the surface story, but they may have even forgotten the true timeline of events that led to their success. I will say it again; trying to compare or stick to a mid-term plan is only going to place unnecessary pressure on you.

I firmly believe that what you put out in to the universe is what you get back. This applies just as much for negativity as it does for positivity. You do not want to be working yourself up into a negative mindset, because this will only attract more negative energy. Remember, when you focus on a yellow car, you are going to see more yellow cars. If you focus on negativity, you are going to be more susceptible to negativity. Daniela Tempesta for Huffpost writes; "[Comparing ourselves to others] requires that we take pleasure in someone else's failures or misfortunes in order to feel adequate, which can fuel mean-spirited competitiveness versus collaboration."(43) If you begin working from a mindset that craves comparison you will be contradicting all of the work that you put in during the prayer stage, and you will further be shorting out your opportunity for growth that will take place in the helping others stage. You cannot compare apples and oranges. I really like this statement because although you might be in the same field as someone else, just as apples and oranges are both fruit, you are not made the same way. You will evolve totally differently. You are different fruit, who can grow in the same garden harmoniously but you must not compare your growth to that of the next person – whether or not they are a mentor or someone you look up to.

That being said, I need you to focus primarily on your own timeline, and more importantly on the goal directly in front of you. Envisioning your future is a great way to keep you motivated but it must not distract you from the here and now. Jay Dixit for *Psychology Today* believes that in order for you to improve your performance in any aspect of your life, you need to stop thinking about it. Overthinking only gives you the feeling that people are constantly on the lookout for your failures, when in fact they are just as busy trying to achieve their own life goals. Besides, those whom are concerned with where you are headed are either loving family members or people whose opinions are irrelevant to your life path. Whichever one of these people worries you is immaterial. What other people think of you is none of your business. Don't attempt to correct them; don't attempt to compare yourself to them. You are only selling yourself short if you do so.

Let it go!

Dixit goes on to explain other key elements of letting go and living in the now. These include: avoid worrying about the future; inhabit the present; make the most of your time by losing track of it; move toward things that bother you rather than away from them; and "know that you don't know."(44)

Know that you don't know.

I like this.

I have mentioned it earlier that you don't know what could possibly come next in your life. We are able to predict what could possibly come next and work towards an environment that is conducive to achieving this, but you do not know for certain. When you are in the flow, that uncertainty gives you peace instead of anxiety. So let go of your worries about the future and immerse yourself in your present day. Don't worry about breaking ground for your school; don't worry about how you are going to manage the down payment on that vacation home; don't worry about everything. It will work itself out now that you are living in the flow and more especially now that you have prepared your mental, spiritual and physical environment to be conducive for it. I want us to move on to why, exactly, it becomes incredibly difficult to plan year-by-year. I need you to look at the world for what it is – beautiful, complex, and chaotic.

◆ ◆ ◆

Every day with every single action we take, we make small, incremental changes to our life path. Trying to plan too far into the future and set deadlines on mid-term goals is incredibly difficult under this notion. Look, nothing is impossible if you set your mind to it, but my purpose is to guide you to a stress-reduced and fulfilling life where your goals work to make your life better not the other way around. These little dynamic events that take place each day shape the outcome of your path. Let's say for instance my cousin's husband had been dead-set on living in Waterloo and declined the job at Amazon; the next stage of his life would not have come to be in a way that was conducive to both he and my cousin's dreams. When you set deadline specific mid-term goals, you miss out on the dynamic changes that could be taking place in your own life; which in turn could be leading you down a different path to success. You become so absorbed by meeting deadlines that your opportunities for growth and success could literally fly over your head without you noticing.

We are currently facing a global pandemic of epic proportions. Businesses have to think on their feet and take each day as it comes. The world over, legal implications and guidelines as per safe operation of almost every single business known to man changes as the knowledge that we have about the virus changes. How do you plan in a climate like this? It's borderline insanity to attempt to foresee where we will be by next month, let alone next year. This serves as just one key example of how at any moment your entire life can change, it just so happens that this example is being played out on a global stage. One day we all went to bed and when we woke up the world had completely changed. This can happen on a much smaller scale in your own life. It doesn't take a pandemic to rock the boat. You could wake up one day and kiss your partner goodbye as they leave for work and not know that it is the last time that you will do so. You could wake up feeling nauseated one morning only to find out the joy of being an expectant mom. Your life would change and shift around your newfound needs. Future deadlines just nine months into the future would have to be shifted and rearranged. Your life is constantly changing – every second of every day. Don't put the pressure on yourself to stick to some timeline that may or may not come to pass.

Commit to the process, don't be consumed by it.

I'll keep saying it.

Just keep living in the present and focus on living a fulfilled life that is open to your impending success, not constantly fighting to achieve your mental version of it. It is vision not version. You foresee it, and you can manifest it, but you cannot control it fully.

Another reason why it is so difficult to set mid-term goals is that we as human beings are primarily spontaneous; we make decisions on the fly, so to speak. We have adapted our minds to take in information at rapid rates, categorize it, and decipher it. As such, humans find it incredibly difficult to plan for mid-term goals. As your environment shifts and changes, your instinct to adapt kicks in. If you have tied yourself to mid-term goals that contradict this change you will find yourself in a position where you are either inclined to give up on your long-term goal or to force the situation, leading to stress - and I have already spoken about your flight-or-fight response to stress. We, as humans, have a very large prefrontal cortex allowing us to use complex languages, to use logic and reason, as well as to make complex decisions. However, in moments of stress your instinctual fight-or-flight response is activated – and while in some cases circumnavigating this response can work to your advantage and reduce your stress; in others it may be best to use this hard-wired response to your benefit. Famed self-help speaker, Bill Stainton says, "[Rather] than try to fight millennia of hard-wiring, let's use it to our advantage. Let's agree that we are, by nature, short-term, reactive creatures. And let's build that into our plans. Yes, make long-term goals. But then break those long-term goals down into numerous short-term goals which, when completed, will also complete the long-term goal."(45) You can be in the flow with your natural instincts and still circumnavigate the stress response by preparing in the short-term. It will allow you to progress through some wins before your brain has the chance to identify another change in its environment. That way when changes do occur, it is easy to assimilate your short-term targets towards this change because they can be actively modified and accomplished within relatively short spaces of time. Think about it this way; you have planned to build your school and you are tempted to set breaking ground as a mid-term goal. Instead of placing the importance on breaking ground in the far future, break it down into smaller actionable steps such as finding a few ideal properties to choose from, finding a potential construction team, deciding on themes and building styles, and so on. That way breaking ground becomes part of a string of smaller actionable goals along the road to achieving your long-term – or core – goal.

The problem with mid-term goals is that with just one small deviation from the plan, you will likely become de-motivated and give up. You cannot place so much importance on achieving a mid-term goal as a pre-requisite for your long-term goal because then it ends up taking precedence over your long-term goal. You will begin to feel as though if you can't accomplish the mid-term goal, it is impossible to accomplish the long-term goal. You could move to another city or even another country in the time between now and a potential mid-term goal. If you place this mid-term goal – like breaking ground for example – in the forefront of your mind you could end up forcing your way to stay in your current city or country. You have become so enveloped by the plan of having this school in this particular town, that you forgot that the core long-term goal was just to have a school. You may have missed out on an opportunity to open the school in another city or country. Perhaps there are even premises that you could purchase in the new city that work out cheaper than what it would have cost to build in your current city. Mid-term planning places precedence on what you believe is the right path based on information that could change at any moment. Don't limit yourself by setting mid-term goals. They suck! If you had been focusing on short-term goals such as researching your business, finding several construction companies that would work well with your design vision, finding potential properties to give you a better idea of building codes and possible future problems; then you would be in a far better position to move to another city and pick up right where you left off, with just a few minor changes as per business policy in that new city. Trying to assess where you will be in a year requires you to have information which you don't even have yet. Don't put yourself in a situation where you end up feeling like you have failed. Let's move on to how you can set challenging but accessible targets. This will allow you to get some quick wins under your belt and it will ultimately help to keep you motivated.

◆ ◆ ◆

I've already spoken about using the SMART acronym to create short-term goals – that means they have to be Specific, Measurable, Attainable, Realistic, and Timely. Let's look at this in a bit more detail now.

In order for your short-term goals to work towards your long-term goal they have to be specific. You need to have a good idea of what it is you are setting out to achieve. For instance, you can set a goal of having your school name decided and trademarked within your first month. You know that in order to do so you will need to research name availability. This is another example of what could be your first short-term goal if you were hoping to open a school. You have made the goal specific. You would also need to be able to measure the goal. Does the goal have meaning? Here you would consider what the school name means to you. Is it derivative of something important in your own life? Perhaps it is a family name which allows you to leave a lasting legacy for your family.

The goal needs to be attainable, so you need to be able to reach the goal with as little resistance as possible. Trying to set a goal to have a name similar to a competitor, for example, makes the goal less likely to be attainable.

The goal needs to be realistic, and something as simple as researching a name and trademarking it is realistic enough.

The goal also needs to be timely, meaning that the goal has to be time based. The problem with making long-term goals in a time based fashion is that, as I said, there is no way of planning that far into the future – only envisioning. Short-term goals allow you the ability to set time boundaries around them because they are easily attainable right away or in the very near future.

You need to define some quick wins; challenging but accessible targets, which will keep you motivated. When you are able to focus on the present it takes the pressure off of focusing on your long-term goal. Think about it this way. When you are studying towards a degree, you are not constantly thinking about obtaining your degree. Your educational journey is broken down into years, and from years into semesters, and from semesters into assignments and tests. Think of your short-term goals as assignments. While you are studying, you are focused on your daily activities of attending classes. You then have short-term goals which may include doing research and completing assignments. This removes the need to constantly focus on your long-term goal of obtaining your degree. You are satisfied by living in the present, knowing that each assignment which you complete brings you one step closer to your degree. Now, I want you to think about mid-term goals as being exams. Amazingly, some exams are even referred to as mid-terms! Think about the stress that focusing on the impending exam can place you under. When you reroute your focus towards doing accurate research, completing assignments and perhaps smaller-scale tests, you are able to live presently and immerse yourself in the information which you will need to successfully complete the upcoming exams. The key is to focus on the short-term, and the rest will take care of itself. There is a reason why we say "I'll cross that bridge when I get to it." This is because you have no idea what the bridge will look like by the time you get there. You can do your best to envision it, but planning for something that can change at any moment – and which you have no control over – is going to wreak havoc on your mental health. Similarly, you have no idea what the exam will entail until your lecturers, or professors, begin exam preparations.

Focusing on mid-term goals gives you far more stress than is necessary; while focusing on short-term goals gives you assignments which you can complete in the here and now.

Working towards short-term goals removes your train of thought from the magnitude of what you are trying to accomplish, and focuses your thoughts on easily attainable milestones that you can achieve relatively quickly. Let's take pregnancy as another example. It is a process of nine months. No matter how anxious you become over the thought of your delivery, no matter how tired and achy your body becomes, no matter how much thought and energy you put into this, your pregnancy will still go on for roughly nine months. Please don't get me wrong, it is important to plan for the arrival of your child to some degree, but let's think about it from the perspective of a woman in her first trimester. At this stage, many women are advised against telling friends and loved ones about their pregnancy because the heartbreaking reality is that, for many women, their pregnancy does not continue past this first trimester. Planning for the second or third trimester at this stage is exciting, and it is a most joyous time, but it comes with some risk. In the most unfortunate event of losing a child in the first trimester - after all the excitement of planning - it could cause severe mental distress and heartbreak for the parents, particularly the mother. Bear in mind that I am using a potentially very sensitive subject of pregnancy as a metaphor. This is not my attempt to advise expectant mothers, as I do not feel that is my place. I am using this metaphor to highlight the uncertainty of life. When you place importance over mid-term goals, instead of short-term goals you set yourself up for potential heartache and disappointment. Similarly, trying to decorate a nursery during the first trimester could prove quite tricky. Perhaps you want to follow some form of traditional color schemes for a boy or a girl, but you are not yet aware of the gender of your baby. This is not to say that pink wouldn't work just as well for a boy as it would for girl, but perhaps that is not what you had envisioned. You would then be repainting walls, bringing in new furnishings, and causing unnecessary strain on yourself. Likewise, you may have a vision for your birthing experience and may even have a birth plan in place. If you are focused solely on this birth plan as your goal, should things not go according to it – which is likely in delivery – you could miss out on the joy of bringing your little one into the world while being focused on the disappointment of not having stuck to your birth plan. In this sense, this is just like mid-term goals. Short-term goals would be making sure you take your prenatal vitamins daily, as well as making sure you are up to date on all your prenatal doctor's appointments. You might even enroll in *Lamaze* classes, yoga or gym classes. These are small, short-term actionable steps that you can take to ensure a healthy and happy birthing experience. I must reiterate; this is not my attempt to advise expectant mothers. I have used these metaphors to show you just how in all aspects of life – and with all goals – there is a level of uncertainty. When you are in the flow, and you focus on short-term goals, you create little wins for yourself that translate to the success of your long-term goal.

This brings us to the next section of this chapter. Short-term goals are small pieces of the big picture. You have already seen how short-term efforts – such as completing assignments – lead to the eventual achievement of obtaining your goal – such as a degree. This is a principle that I want you to be aware of and take on in your life. All the small efforts that you make in the present will edge you closer to your dreams, and lifelong success. As they say, the devil is in the detail.

◆ ◆ ◆

Let's take a literal picture as an example here – or a painting rather. Say you want to create a realistic painting of a mountain. You are not just going to paint the mountain are you? You are going to paint the sky; perhaps some clouds; the sun; and maybe even snow or grass. You may even paint people frolicking around in the grass or snow. You will have a vision of whether you are going to be painting snowcapped mountains, or jagged volcanic rock. All of these tiny details, such as the time of day, the season, or the weather, will form part of your picture. The point is that you are going to have much smaller details in mind which will tell you what color palettes to use, the size of your canvas, and so on. Do you see just how important these small details are in creating the bigger picture? As I mentioned, your short-term goals are part of the bigger picture, without them you have no bigger picture. These little details form the basis of the outcome of what you are trying to achieve. You know that you are going to end up with a picture of a mountain, but will it be an island setting or a snowy setting? Just as we have looked at the prospect of leaving your city and moving to another, that detail, or short-term action, doesn't have to stop you from having your dream come true. It will just change the background over which it takes place – in essence your island or your snowy wilderness. This is why envisioning your long-term, core goal was of such importance. It will help to guide you in terms of setting your short-term goals – or picking your color palette and setting. This vision will act as your guide, but as you progress with your painting, the image may take shape in a different way than expected. Remember that in life you only get one canvas. You cannot throw it away and start with a new one, but you can incorporate the little smudges and errors as you paint to form a beautiful picture. There is no reset button in life, but if you can roll with the punches along the way, you will be able to incorporate all of the little miss-steps.

Mid-term goals give you a feeling of failure when they fall through. Short-term goals assure you that everything is a part of the bigger picture. There are no failures – only detours and life lessons.

Everything that is of consequence in your life happens in the short-term – the way in which your mind processed an interview question in a split second which led to you getting the job; the moments that it took for you to run late just long enough to miss a three lane pile up on your route to work. You can envision the future but you do not live there. You live here – right now as you read this book. This is where your focus should be. You may take away all of the concepts written in this book, or you could very well be impacted by one small statement. That little piece of the big picture which this book represents is all that it might take to ignite change within you – to inspire you. I have heard so many stories of how people were inspired by their grade school teachers and how one small statement in a classroom during the course of their youth is the reason why they chose the career that they did. This is because as children we still embrace the little details. We still fall in love with the mystical 'magic' of a helium filled balloon. It is so important to see the world with childlike optimism as you progress through your journey in life. Revel in the mystery of all the tiny details that surround your life.

Focus on the present.

Embrace your short-term goals to achieve your long-term success.

People may argue that focusing on mid-term goals as opposed to short-term goals alleviates the strain of being in a revolving door of constant goals, but mid-term goals are just the middleman. Let's cut the middleman out for a second. Whether or not mid-term goals are present, you will always need short-term goals to achieve your long-term goal. When we dig in to eat a pizza, we don't just grab the whole thing and start chewing on the crust. That's madness. You cut a pizza up into smaller pieces that you can easily enjoy. It's important to see the big picture for what it is – the sum of the details. Just as the pizza is cut into manageable pieces, your long-term goal is achieved in 'bite-size' pieces.

Life is full of wonder and it is only our need for control which robs us of the excitement of the unknown. As you begin to let go of this need for control, you are able to experience the excitement of the present. You are able to appreciate all of life's ups and downs as being part of your journey. You begin to develop a mindset that not only sees the positive in almost all situations, but actively seeks the positive out. It is your life to live. Give yourself a pat on the back when you accomplish a short-term goal. Give yourself a reward on top of the reward of succeeding. Double up on the positivity of the small wins in order to keep yourself motivated. When you let go of wanting to know what comes much later in the process you will be able to take the wins as a celebratory milestone, and the so-called 'losses' will be easier to navigate. In the grand scheme of things, time is your most valuable resource. Short-term goals – and their ability to increase productivity and limit procrastination – save you so much time on your journey to your long-term goal. Due to the fact that you are able to have tangible wins in the short-term, you are boosted towards working faster and achieving your long-term goal in a shorter space of time. Your mind is already hard-wired towards achieving your long term goal. You don't have to continually focus on it for it to be achieved. Your ability to envision and dream without boundaries is what will guide your short-term goal setting. You don't need to worry that you will get lost along the way or lose sight of your vision. Trust me, you have put so much effort into creating your vision that your mind will find the ways in which to see it through – and this fact will be highlighted as you set your short-term goals.

We are about to move on to the last section of letting go. I want to circle back to the reference to your life being like a car. Everything has to work in unison and be in constant balance. If you tip the scales in any direction, your car is not going to go anywhere. The process is all about letting go of control and living in the present, while simultaneously setting short-term goals that ensure you are on the right path.

Not too much control, not too much slack – balance.

Similarly, your long-term goal can be linked to the metaphor of a car journey. Let me clarify – your long-term goal is the destination of your car journey. Your short-term goals are the milestones along the way – all of these seemingly small strides which get you from Point A to Point B. I want you to remember this reference of your life being like a car and go back to the Introduction section if you must.

Now let's move on to this car journey.

❖ ❖ ❖

Suppose you want to go on vacation, and you want it to be a road trip. You know that you are traveling from your home to a specific vacation property. You know your destination but you don't know all the details of the entire route to get there. You envision this journey and prepare for it. You do a little research to immerse your mental plane in images of what it might be like when you arrive. You pray for safe travels and give thanks for the wonderful vacation you are heading out on. You let go of the worry over safe travels and you set out.

As you begin your journey, you start off only being able to see just 100 meters ahead of your car. With every meter you progress, you see one more meter of the road ahead of you, and so it goes on. You take in the sights and sounds as you progress on your journey. The landscapes change and perhaps even the weather, too. You enjoy a light meal as you stop to stretch your legs and take in the warm air.

This is your life.

You don't know what is up ahead on that road. You can see for some distance in front of you and this is the distance which you plan for. The little bit which you can see in front of you is the distance you navigate, until you can see a little further and a little further after that. You focus on the journey and take in all of the little details that you can see through your window. The small things that you can do to prepare like packing some snacks; filling your tires with air; making sure your oil and water is topped up; and filling up with gas are all short-term actions that you can take in the present to help you progress on your journey. When you look back on the trip, you will have fond memories of the drive itself and not just the destination. This is because the short-term, and seemingly inconsequential, actions that we take every day lead to the bigger picture. How you choose to set these short-term goals and engage with them will determine your ability to sustain your happiness in the long run. It will also determine the likelihood of you achieving your long-term goal.

There may be an unforeseen road-block on the way. You may burst a tire and you will also likely need to stop for gas, or to use the restroom. These minor changes to the timeline of your arrival don't stop you from reaching your destination. These details form a part of your journey and the bigger picture; but they are often there in aid of the bigger picture. You wouldn't turn your car around and head back home just because you had to stop for gas. You also wouldn't turn your car around and head back home because you didn't arrive at the vacation property exactly when you expected to. So why would you do that on your life's journey? All the little details – whether convenient or inconvenient in the moment – are part of the bigger picture and they have purpose in the grand scheme of your life path. Your short-term goals are like road markers that help you see how far you have come.

◆ ◆ ◆

Let's recap the Let it Go stage before moving on to Chapter Five – Helping Others. I know that it may seem counter-productive to let your dream go, but it is the exact opposite. You have done most of the work that needs to be done in moving towards achieving your goals. If you hold on to your goals too tightly you can become consumed by them. Maintaining focus and motivation is not the same as being obsessed about something; and being obsessed is a sure-fire way to cloud your mind and make rash and impulsive decisions. Your goal will always be in the forefront of what you do because you have gone through all the necessary previous steps to cement this. What you should be focusing on at this stage are your short-term goals. Focus on placing one foot in front of the other on your journey now.

Your short-term goals should be aligned with your vision, and you will be able to achieve this by revisiting your vision board whenever you feel the need to. Remember, focus does not mean obsession, so do this sporadically. Short-term goals keep you motivated; mid-term goals suck! Mid-term goals generally run from six months to three years to achieve. Setting mid-term goals can add to your stress because as your environment constantly changes, your mid-term goals are likely to be rendered redundant long before you have gotten close to achieving them.

It is far too complicated to plan year by year up to the point that you reach your ultimate goal. When you set a long-term goal, the likelihood is that the goal involves something that you have never achieved before – otherwise you wouldn't be placing this much importance on it. You can research as much as you would like to, but the path will change along the way. Your immersive research as well as surrounding yourself with information in support of your goal is only to motivate you in the fact that it can be done. This immersive technique is only there to help you envision what can be achieved. It is not there to inform you of what each year of the process will look like. Of course, you can look to people whom have achieved what you are setting out to achieve for inspiration, but you cannot compare the timeline of their success to plan your own.

Every day with every single action we take, we make small, incremental changes to our life path. Trying to envision too far into the future and set deadlines on mid-term goals is incredibly difficult under this notion. These little dynamic events that take place each day shape the outcome of your path. When you set deadline specific mid-term goals, you miss out on the dynamic changes which could be leading you down a different path to success. You become so absorbed by meeting deadlines that your opportunities for growth and success could literally fly over your head without you noticing.

Once you are able to let go, make your short-term goals SMART. In order for your short-term goals to work towards your long-term goal they have to be specific. You need to have a good idea of what it is you are setting out to achieve. You would also need to be able to measure the goal. The goal needs to have meaning and it also needs to be attainable; so you need to be able to reach the goal with as little resistance as possible. The goal needs to be realistic. While your long-term goal – and subsequent vision – should not be bound by what your current reality dictates; your short-term goals should ideally be achievable within your current reality. The goal also needs to be timely – meaning that the goal has to be time based. The problem with making long-term goals in a time based fashion is that there is no way of planning so far into the future – only envisioning. Short-term goals allow you the ability to set time boundaries around them because they are easily attainable right away or in the very near future.

If you wanted to create a realistic painting of a mountain, for example, you are not just going to paint the mountain alone. You are going to paint the sky; perhaps some clouds; the sun; and maybe even snow or grass. You may even paint people frolicking around in the grass or snow. You will have a vision of whether you are going to be painting a winter or a summer setting. All of these tiny details, such as the time of day, the season, or the weather, will form part of your picture. The point is that you are going to have much smaller details in mind which will tell you what color palettes to use, the size of your canvas and so on. These small details – or your short-term goals – are a part of the bigger picture. Without them you have no bigger picture. These little details form the basis of the outcome of what you are trying to achieve. This is why envisioning your long-term, core goal was of such importance. It will help to guide you in terms of setting your short-term goals – or picking your color palette and setting.

If you decided to go on a road trip, you would be aware that you are traveling from your home to a specific vacation property. You know your destination but you don't know all the details of the entire route to get there. You envision this journey. You do a little research to immerse your mental plane in images of what it might be like when you arrive. You pray for safe travels and give thanks for the wonderful vacation you are heading out on. You let go of the worry over safe travels and you set out. As you begin your journey, you start off only being able to see just 100 meters ahead of your car. With every meter you progress, you see one more meter of the road ahead of you, and so on. You take in the sights and sounds as you progress on your journey. The landscapes change and perhaps even the weather, too. You enjoy a light meal as you stop to stretch your legs and take in the warm air. This is your life. You don't know what is up ahead on that road. You can see for some distance in front of you and this will be the distance which you plan for. The road ahead is the distance which you navigate, until you can see a little further and a little further after that. You focus on the short-term actions that you can take in the present to help you progress on your journey.

◆ ◆ ◆

You can reap incredible rewards by letting go of the notion that you must cling tightly to your dream in order for it to come to be. Trust me, I have lived it. I once had the opportunity to view the power of letting go and the destruction of holding on for myself. *Some time back, I had invested a bit of money in the crypto currency market. I had done so rather excitedly, and I was eager to make a good return on my investment. I allowed this idea of profitability and success to consume me at a very deep level. Every day I would check in on the value of my investment. As the days rolled on, I began checking on it every hour; and eventually, I got to a point where I was monitoring my investment minute by minute. I was obsessed!*

Now at the very same time that I had invested money into crypto currency, I had also purchased a quarter of an acre of land in the countryside. I had dreams to build a villa there one day; but I had also thought that it might make me a small profit should I choose to sell it in the future. I didn't worry much about that property; it wasn't going anywhere and I knew that its value wouldn't increase for some time. I had mentally let it go.

On the other hand, my obsession with the performance of my crypto currency investment was growing. It had reached a point where it was affecting my mood. I found myself upset whenever its value would drop and excited whenever the value increased. I spent nights lying awake, staring at my mobile screen – just mindlessly watching the zigzagging price pattern. I was constantly anxious and always waiting for the next price drop. I wasn't even at peace when it was on the uptrend. I had this incredible fear of missing out on a big-ticket sale, and as a result I held back from selling when the prices were high – always thinking that they would climb higher. The price value of my investment eventually entered a downtrend, and I was thrown into a mental living-hell. I watched as the price decreased bit by bit, never climbing above its last peak, until I eventually decided to sell far below the purchase value. I exited the market bitterly disappointed and saddened by my losses. The land which I had purchased was the furthest thing from my mind.

Just over a year had passed since my crypto currency disappointment and I decided to go back to the land which I had purchased, and check it out. I then decided to find out about the value of my land only to find out that the municipality had signed off on a new economic-boosting strategy for the area. A proposal to turn the area into a tourist hotspot had been approved and people were flocking to the area to buy land. The prices had soared since that announcement and my property value had tripled quite quickly. I had this goal to make smart profit-rendering investments; but I had so heavily romanticized the thought of making it big with crypto currency, that I had almost overlooked the positive outcome of my property investment. What I had obsessed over, I smothered – and it led to financial fallout. What I had let go, had flourished all on its own – and it led to financial gain. I was so focused on achieving my goal in my own way that I lost sight of the fact that the universe would align itself towards my success – just not in the way that I had planned for it.

This is the power of letting go. Once the seed of your vision is planted, don't dig it up every day to check if it's growing. Let it be, and have faith that although it won't sprout and fruit tomorrow, it will eventually – and when it does, it will change your life.

❖ ❖ ❖

Now it is time to move on to our final chapter. In Chapter Five I am going to introduce you to the concept of helping others. I want you to keep in mind that your core reason for helping others should always be for the good of helping them. Living a purposeful life, paying it forward, giving back and karma are all elements that I will be explaining to you in greater detail. Let's finish strong.

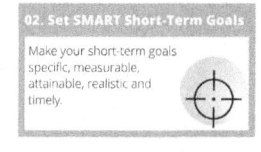

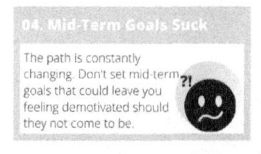

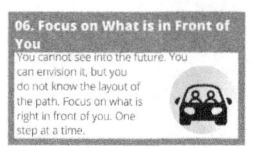

The Letting Go Stage: Setting Your Mind Free

Recap the steps you need to take in order to set your mind free during the letting go stage.

01. Let It Go
Let go of the need to control and obsess over your long-term goal.

02. Set SMART Short-Term Goals
Make your short-term goals specific, measurable, attainable, realistic and timely.

03. Stay in Your Lane
Look to others for inspiration but don't compare the timeline of your progress to theirs.

04. Mid-Term Goals Suck
The path is constantly changing. Don't set mid-term goals that could leave you feeling demotivated should they not come to be.

05. The Details are Part of the Bigger Picture
Every seemingly small action we take leads to the eventual bigger picture of your life. Live in the now and plan for the short-term.

06. Focus on What is in Front of You
You cannot see into the future. You can envision it, but you do not know the layout of the path. Focus on what is right in front of you. One step at a time.

HELPING OTHERS

The power of reciprocity

So you've mastered the art of letting go of full control over your dream. You've put it out into the universe, or to your higher power, and you are happily getting on with your daily affirmations. You are focusing on living a fulfilled and balanced life, with particular attention being paid to the parts of the "car" which represents your life that we looked at way back in the Introduction. Now you will want to add value to this balance. Living a life of purpose and in service of others is something that we should all strive to do. If everyone looked out for everyone else, eventually the good deeds would roll back around. The karmic effect of paying it forward will be looked at in greater detail a little later on this chapter. For now, I want to focus on the impact that giving out of the kindness of your heart can have on your life.

In this section of hyper-goal setting for lifelong success, I want you to embrace the idea of helping others. Don't let extrinsic motivators be your main guide at this stage. Allow intrinsic motivation and the joys of paying it forward guide you as to whom you should help and how you should help them. I'm sure you have heard of the theory that by helping others, you attract the right energy into your sphere which in turn can help you. I don't want this to be your primary focus. Instead the 'karma' of what you receive by doing a good deed should only play a small role in why you are actually doing this good deed – otherwise it is all for nothing. Disingenuous motives are easy to tell from a mile away and that is not the energy that you want to be putting out into the universe. It is also not something you want to look back on in your life and feel regret towards.

Helping others can have a deep impact on your happiness and your confidence. Being able to tell yourself that you are a genuine person who commits to helping others for the right reasons is a great way to live a life of purpose with an elevated conscience. According to Time Magazine; "Scientific research provides compelling data to support the anecdotal evidence that giving is a powerful pathway to personal growth and lasting happiness. Through fMRI technology, we now know that giving activates the same parts of the brain that are stimulated by food and sex." (46) We derive great pleasure out of giving to others; the facts are quite clear on this. You can double down on this effect simply by giving within areas of your own personal interests or values. If you have a particular passion for working with animals, for example, volunteering your time at an animal shelter could foster this feeling of joy and fulfillment. How perfect is it to be able to give back and to bring yourself some much needed joy? Everyone is winning in this situation. Wherever your passion lies, your helping-hand must come from a place of willingness. The last thing I want is for you to feel guilt-tripped into helping others, or pressured in any way by reading this book. Your acts of kindness are not limited to the outside world; as they say, charity begins at home. Taking on an act of service for one of your loved ones could be a simple, but nonetheless profound, way to activate your feelings of fulfillment and purpose.

Boosting your sense of intrinsic motivation and adding value to your balanced life is a way to expedite your success while still maintaining a positive mindset. Marianna Pogosyan Ph.D. writes; "The *well-being-boosting* and *depression-lowering* benefits of volunteering have been repeatedly documented." (47)

What better way is there to alleviate the strain of some of the difficulties that you may be presented with on your journey to success than to do good for others? A giving hand is a receiving hand, so give yourself the gift of fulfillment. I have to warn you not be self-righteous in your actions; rather be humble and be passionate about the avenues in which you are giving. If you go about helping others this way, I promise you will reap the rewards even long after you have reached your goals.

When I say help others with good intentions I also want to refer this to the manner in which you help others. Helping a loved one just to throw it in their face at a later stage does not do one shred of good for them or for you. They will end up resenting you for it and you will end up with a feeling of self-loathing and regret for having done that. Do not act in service of your loved ones only for you to dangle it over them like some sort of trophy. You must engage with everyone around you with a sense of humility. Similarly, helping those that are less fortunate than you only for you to document it for bragging rights is not the way to go. Treating anyone with less dignity than you would expect for yourself is not harnessing the power of reciprocity. In fact, it can have quite a counterintuitive effect and, if you believe in bad karma, this is a tried and tested way to attract some bad karma. Carry out good deeds for the good of it and not for the image. This is another area where keeping it to yourself would be a good idea. Helping someone doesn't have to be a secret, but you don't have to hang a billboard up about it either. Now, this is not to say that you cannot motivate others around you to become helpful by highlighting some of the work you've put in and how it has uplifted you; you can absolutely share this motivation with the world. It all comes down to how you are going about doing it, and why you are doing it. If you feel hesitant to share your good deeds with the world because you feel that you are only doing it to garner attention, that is your conscience speaking – listen to it. If you are sharing your good deeds with the world to give some much needed positivity in what are some very trying times, then you should absolutely go for it. If your aim is to inspire others to do some good deeds, where is the harm? So remember, if it's to brag – keep it to yourself. If it's inspirational – share away.

That being said, there is a way to expedite your success by helping others. By engaging with the community around you, you are also opening yourself up to meeting people who can help you to achieve your dreams. People are also more inclined to help you if you are viewed as someone who helps others. Everyone loves to be a part of a positive success story, particularly if the person achieving the success is someone that the community can look up to. Not only will you be doing something good for others, you will also be creating a whole new network system of connectedness. Bianca Miller Cole for *Forbes Women*, writes, "The contacts you keep are largely attributed to your growth. They largely influence growth in your status and pave the way for better opportunities in your career. Your connections are powerful!" (48) The connections that you form along the way as you fundraise for projects that are close to your heart, or as you engage in volunteer sessions, can ultimately help to shape the path that your dreams take. This will also add substance to your values and create a life of doing, instead of a life of just thinking. These deep and meaningful connections will also likely become a great support system of people to talk to and seek advice from in moments of difficulty.

Helping others can also open your mind up to the way you view the world. As you begin to come across people living through a wide variety of different lifestyles, you are likely to alter the way you view the world - and perhaps even yourself.

This is an opportunity for major spiritual and emotional growth.

Having a mental, emotional and spiritual depth as you pursue your goals is undoubtedly a strong weapon to have in your arsenal. It will allow you to tap into your own inner strengths as you navigate your path to success. Having a mind that is able to accommodate and accept differing opinions will help you to remain fluid and be in the flow of things. As you have already read in Chapter Two, having a growth-mindset as opposed to a rigid mindset is what will help you to shape your dreams. You need to be a person that is able to adapt with the times. This is not only a survival trait, but a trait that many successful people share.

Not only can helping others help to shape your own growth-mindset, it can also provide you with a wealth of knowledge as you engage with many different people from all walks of life. Humans are like walking libraries, and the older we get the more of a wealth of knowledge we possess. The life experiences and technical knowledge possessed by the people you will come into contact with will expose you to hundreds of living libraries. When you open yourself up to learning from others irrespective of age, social status or anything else that is immaterial, you allow yourself the opportunity to make informed decisions that you may not have been able to make on your own. In order to achieve something that you are passionate about, but that you may have limited experience in, you should tap into the experiences of others. Operating an animal shelter might be worlds apart from operating a school, but at the core they are both businesses – one for profit and one not for profit. The legal concerns in hiring staff and taking on volunteers, is something that the shelter operator or coordinator could help to advise you on. They may have some wisdom on financial management as they have to be incredibly frugal in managing donated budgets. This is just one of an endless amount of outcomes that could come to fruition as a result of helping others and opening yourself up to learning from them in the process. All you have to do is be open, be creative, and be willing in the way that you interact with the people around you. If you do this, you will be able to expedite your own dreams by helping others.

This brings me to the point of paying it forward. This literary concept is so widely accepted that it has even been used to create film adaptations and fan-fiction short stories. Let's move on to this concept now.

◆ ◆ ◆

When you have helped others, be gracious in the help that you have offered them. Don't expect anything in return; instead encourage them to pay it forward. Paying it forward is the act of passing on the kindness that someone has shown you instead of working towards returning the favor. This frees the person, whom you have helped, up from the stress or time-constrained pressure of returning the favor to you, and opens them up to the joy of helping someone else. If everyone worked towards paying it forward it would create a global atmosphere for change – one where each person has access to the help they need from those around them. Sometimes it is the smallest acts of random kindness that can save a person from a dark and desperate situation. Fostering this sense of giving and connectedness not only uplifts your own spirit, but triggers a chain of events that could come back to you in the most positive way.

By shifting your focus from your own needs to the needs of others, it can help you to gain perspective on your own situation. More often than not we doubt our strength and capabilities. We feel as though we carry the weight of the world on our shoulders. During times of your own personal difficulty, when you help someone - whether you're paying forward the kindness you have received or not - it helps you to realize that maybe things aren't as bad for you as you thought they were. When you realize how capable you are of igniting change around you and positively impacting your community, you will reaffirm your purpose and wash away feelings of self-pity or negativity. By helping others, you are ultimately also helping yourself.

When it comes to the theory of paying it forward, Milena Tsvetkova and Michael Macy write for the New York Times; "[Generosity] among strangers can be socially contagious. According to this theory, if you receive or observe an act of help, you become more likely to help others, even if your own action won't be directly reciprocated or rewarded." (49) Your one act of generosity is enough to set off a ripple effect of generosity that will be felt throughout your community. When you put positivity out into the world, it will find its way back to you. However small your act of generosity may be, if it comes from a place of sincerity you will have a positive impact on the world around you. Even if nothing comes of this right away, wouldn't it be better to live in a community that is a little bit better off than what it was before you set out to help? Wouldn't this in itself be an uplifting reminder of what an impact that small incremental actions, such as the short-term goals you had set, can have? I most certainly think it would; in fact, I know that it would. I am not one to preach and not practice and this is the reason why I give you a story from my own life at the end of each chapter. Hold tight for it – and don't skip to the end to find out how helping others impacted my life.

So how can you pay it forward, and how can you encourage others to pay it forward?

It starts with the little things.

You just have to be in tune with yourself and your environment in order to notice them. Let's say you are sitting in traffic. There's an obstruction up ahead in your lane, and your lane has ground to a halt. You're already running a little late for work but you are now living in the flow of things and have told yourself that this is an unforeseeable circumstance that you cannot change – so you're not too stressed about it. You signal to merge into the next lane and car after car crawls past you with no intent of letting you in. You're feeling a little frustrated now, but you keep calm. Eventually the car behind you signals for you to merge. You're so grateful to be moving again. That person may have been let in a little further back, and they are now paying it forward.

Now it's your turn.

You're on your lunch break and you see a woman anxiously looking at her watch as she is in the back of the line waiting to place an order at your local eatery. You notice this and decide it's time to pay it forward. You yell over to her and ask her what she's having. She replies and you place her order for her. She thanks you and offers to pay you back, but you tell her to pay it forward instead. Days go by and you've long forgotten about the chain of events that led to you helping that lady during your lunch break, but you notice as you walk out of a meeting that someone has paid your parking meter. Your meeting had gone on a while longer than expected and you had prepared yourself for a parking citation.

Could it be that someone in your pay-it-forward chain paid the meter for you?

It is quite possible.

I think you are starting to see how the process of paying it forward can have a ripple effect on your environment, but can it also have a snowball effect? It sure can. The generosity can pick up steam and before you know it, that one act of kindness that was shown to you in peak traffic has snowballed into something much bigger. If we all focused on being in the flow; living in a stress reduced manner; and paying it forward, there would be far-reaching positive effects not only for us but for our communities as well.

I want you to practice living in the now and making a conscious effort to pay it forward whenever and wherever you can. It is in the little actions and the fleeting moments that our lives can be shaped and changed for the better. This is another reason why short-term goals are more important than mid-term goals when it comes to achieving your long-term goal. It is due to the fact that your life changes with every small decision you make. Therefore, the briefness of a short-term goal by comparison to the length of your lifespan aligns itself with the briefness that it takes for your life to be changed forever. Everything happens in the now, and in the short-term. Now, although these short-term fleeting moments are important in shaping the way your future plays out, it's incredibly important not to take this as a sign to obsess over the little things. Many people, who tend to fixate, often hear this as an opportunity to take back control of some sort. I am going to tell you now that it is just the opposite. You cannot fixate on your short-term goals and on every small decision that you make in order to see your long-term goal through; you will burn out. The only reason why it is important for you to know that your daily decisions and manner of doing things affects your life path is for you to realize that you cannot possibly control everything. I am telling you this because I need to bolster the belief in you that when you let things go, as we have discovered in Chapter Four, things work out for the better. Just as you have learned to let go in the previous chapter, you also need to learn to let go as you move forward with helping others. Don't expect some reward or praise for doing what you are doing, just focus on how uplifted you feel when you are helping others. Focus on being present and living with gratitude towards the fact that you are fortunate enough to be able to lend a helping hand. You have to be able to take pleasure in the possibility that your acts of kindness could have ripple effects so far that it could potentially save someone's life; somewhere down your pay-it-forward chain.

When you are able to feel as though you are a valuable member of society – and please remember that you always are, no matter what – you will exude a more positive demeanor. I want you to start working on ways to help others today and when you do I want you to take note of your energy levels, your posture, your manner of speaking, and your overall wellbeing. These are some of the noticeable facets of your life that will start to change for the better. You will be walking taller, breathing deeper, speaking with conviction, feeling grateful and radiating a sense of purpose in life. When you pay it forward, you are giving to others without expecting to receive anything in return. You are giving wholly from the goodness of your heart, and you know by now how important it is to listen to your heart. Some studies have shown that this servant-mindset, or living in service of others, has had amazing benefits on chronic pain sufferers. As they began helping others, their minds gradually shifted away from their own pain receptors to the needs of others. Isn't that just amazing? You are able to boost your own health and morale just by being a giving and open person.

Perhaps the most obvious of ways that this form of helping others helps you is that you are able to engage with a diverse group of people, and this sense of connectedness can greatly reduce your stress levels. We will look at this a little deeper in the sections to follow, but for now I want to talk to you very briefly about how helping others can remove you from a feeling of loneliness and isolation. On one hand, you could possibly be a lone wolf in life and as such tend to withdraw and feel a bit isolated from the world at times. On the other hand, you could be incredibly extroverted but are afraid to be your true self around others, leaving you with a sense of loneliness once the charade is over. Look, we all wear different hats for the different roles we have in life and many of us tend to want to conform in order to reduce the stress of standing out too much. It is a detrimental psychological survival technique, and one that you can curb by helping others. You will help yourself via your connectedness to transparent people, who want nothing from you but your time to help. You will be able to be your most authentic self and this acceptance amongst peer volunteers and those whom you are helping will boost your confidence to a point where you no longer feel the need to conform. You will be able to stand out as the wonderfully unique individual that you are and you will be able to unlock certain facets of your personality that you had long forgotten – or perhaps never even knew existed.

You will be able to really and deeply feel again.

Your happiness is such a pivotal part of your success in life. Anything that brings you material gain, but steals your joy is not worth its weight in gold. Paying it forward creates an environment conducive to your personal growth; to your success journey; and to your happiness. Let's unpack this with a little more depth.

◆ ◆ ◆

I've touched very briefly on how helping others can boost your own happiness, but let's look at this in a bit more detail. When you live a life in service of others, it serves as a great source of fulfillment and motivation. Not only this, but it serves as a healthy alternative to the distractions which we fill our lives with. Have you ever been feeling a little stressed out and you immediately pick up your phone and scroll through social media to numb your mind and pass the time? The majority of us have done it at least once before. Now here's the problem with that. Being on social media constantly can compound your feelings of stress. Remember how comparing yourself to others can have a negative impact on your mental health? Well, the internet – and social media in particular – is the biggest melting pot for easily accessible comparison to your peers or mentors.

TV isn't any better these days either.

There's a constant barrage of self-image driven products being advertised to us, telling us how imperfect we are and what we need to buy in order to fix ourselves. The news seems like it is always bad news lately, and while it is important to be abreast of what is going on around you, it is equally important not to become consumed by it. Switching off from the tech for a moment and getting out to actively participate in events where you can make a measurable difference, not only boosts your morale but offers a much needed break and distraction from your own life momentarily – that is far better than being distracted by TV or the internet. Don't get me wrong, living in the now and being present in your life is a way to be fulfilled, and helping others is a definite way to do this. When I speak of distraction, I'm not speaking of becoming mindless in the moment; I'm speaking of becoming mindful outside the realm of your own self momentarily.

On the topic of pass times, I want you to create a habit out of helping others to the point that it becomes an enjoyable hobby. Make it a part of your weekly routine and be sure to engage in philanthropic activities that resonate with your core values and passions. Many of us become so bogged down in trying to achieve what we perceive to be the next phase of our lives that we forget to stop and really live in the moment. Filling your time with meaningful connections and interactions ensures that you constantly feel as though you are living in the moment. This is a great example of just how helping others can improve your own happiness and boost feelings of fulfillment. It doesn't matter what age you are, whether you are single or in a committed relationship, or whether or not you have children – helping others is a great way to add value to your own life in a positive way.

Let's touch on this for a moment.

We have looked at how my method of hyper-goal setting can also be applicable to your personal life. It does not have to revolve around just career, business, or financial goals. Perhaps you are at a point where you are ready to meet someone. In a fast paced world where everyone is constantly online and everyone is looking for a 'hook-up' instead of something deeper, looking for a partner out in a club, on social media, or at a bar is probably going to mean that you have to go through quite a lot of trial and error before you can meet someone that matches you. This is not to say that many people have not met their loved ones in this manner – they have, and many are happily married and going strong. However, if this is the method you have used in the past and it has failed you relentlessly, maybe it is time to take a different approach. Getting out into your community and engaging in activities to help others via avenues that are close to your heart is a fantastic way to meet someone that is suited to you.

How so?

You are not intoxicated, you are not in a loud and interfering environment, and you know that the person whom you are engaging with has similar core values as you – they are volunteering somewhere that resonates with your own core values. There is no social media façade, no filters and angled photos, just a person whom is similar to you in their natural form. A great bonus is that you are in a safe environment and chances are you all have had to sign a volunteer roster or fill out forms which ensures your safety from potential predators – which let's face it is a frightening but all too real prospect nowadays, especially in bars or on social media. If nothing comes of it, one thing you will at least be able to say is that you may have made a lifelong friend and a confidant with similar values as yours.

If you are married and perhaps have children, helping others is also a great way to incorporate them in worthwhile family activities. Children whom are exposed to the notion of philanthropy at a young age have a better understanding of the world around them much sooner than those who aren't. This is wonderful opportunity to teach your children some much needed life lessons as well as having them view their parents in a different light. Children, particularly teenagers, are also quite susceptible to falling into the technology 'fly-trap'. Gadgets and social media can consume teens and become particularly unhealthy in terms of their mental wellbeing – but it also makes them more susceptible to age inappropriate material, predators and bullies. Helping others allows you to create environments where your children can learn to engage with people of all ages and from all walks of life in a respectful and safe manner. If it boosts your self-confidence and sense of purpose, imagine what it can do for your children at a young and impressionable age. Having a safe and fulfilling outlet for children is a definite bonus of helping others and engaging in regular philanthropic activities. It is a known fact that children thrive off of positive routine.

Perhaps you are in a happily committed relationship but there are no children in the picture. Helping others can cement a deep respect for one another as you get to view each other in a new and positive light. Couples who share core values and actively engage in activities that resonate with these values have longer lasting and more meaningful relationships as opposed to those who don't. It opens up new pathways for communication and helps each party to appreciate the other for whom they are, outside of the relationship. The Optimist by 'Goz Around' has shared their *Five Reasons Why You Should Volunteer as a Couple*. "It's a Powerful Bonding Experience; You Discover Your Shared Values; You Try New Things; You Count Your Blessings; and You Double Your Impact in the Community." (50) You are able to try out new things as a couple; giving more depth and meaning to your relationship. On the other side of that very same coin, it is also a way to iron out uncertainties regarding your partner's personality and values.

Are these the early days of your relationship?

Are they really a match for you?

These are questions that may be burning in your mind and perhaps you will be able to pick up on certain faux pas that you would not have under mundane circumstances at home. It is very easy to pick up on whether or not someone is genuinely who they say they are in volunteer type settings. As I mentioned, it is a sad truth, but truth nonetheless – not everyone who comes into your life is meant to stay, at least not in the original role they've played. Getting out and helping others, not only helps those in need but can also help you to expedite the process of figuring out whether or not the person you have taken a shine to is really on your wave length.

If you are kicking a bad habit or even something more severe such as an addiction engaging with people who suffer similar afflictions could help you to achieve this goal. There is a good reason why groups such as Alcoholics Anonymous offer some type of peer system and sponsors to keep everyone on the right path to recovery. This is because when we do things of this magnitude in larger groups instead of trying to resolve the matter alone, we are more likely to succeed. The reciprocal support that you can gain from helping others in this aspect is almost instantaneous and it is an excellent intrinsic motivator to help others – and perhaps to achieve a core goal of kicking an addiction, or a lesser habit. Removing yourself from groups of people and environments that remind you of habit forming behavior will help you to set off on a path to recovery.

What is the best way to do that?

I believe that the best way to do this is to place yourself amongst people, and within environments, that offer the opposite effect. Remove yourself from the bar scene and throw yourself into some voluntary work. Listen very carefully, because I need you to understand that replacing one vice with another – whether or not it is healthy for you – can be a slippery slope into relapse. However, it is a good starting point to clear your mind long enough, and enrich your life by helping others, in order to progress towards getting the long-term help that you need. This is not a topic I take very lightly, and if you are in need of help start by talking to someone. You can contact anyone of your national substance abuse hotlines. You can find numbers for Canadian and American hotlines at the link in the Bibliography Section (H:1). As I mentioned charity begins at home. It may be you, yourself, who needs that charity first. If things have become quite serious for you, please reach out. There are so many of us out there who are ready and willing to help; or to just hold space with you in silence; and just listen if that is what you need. If you feel that you are going through something that you can overcome without intervention, I highly suggest getting out of old habits by beginning to help others. I promise you that it will spark a change in you that will be deep and long-lasting. By putting the needs of others before your own – even if only over short, routine periods of time – you will allow yourself the clarity to realize just how amazing you truly are.

I want us to look some more defining factors in helping others: karma and praying for others. I have left these two points until last because I believe that you should be motivated to help others for the good of helping them, and not just for the reward. However, that being said, I do believe that there are karmic rewards to helping others.

Let's have a look.

◆ ◆ ◆

    Have you ever been in a fierce mood and you feel like your day is going horribly wrong, making your general demeanor towards others less than kind?

Yes?

    In one of those moments, have you ever tried to storm out of a room only for your shirt or jacket sleeve to get caught on the door handle on the way out – immediately deflating your hot head? For many people around the world, this is what they believe to be karma in action. Now karma is not always instantaneous, sometimes it takes a while to roll back around – but it does come back around. In this section I want to talk you to a little more on the positive effects of karma, or good karma, and how you can build up some of it in your life just by helping others.

    Hugh Warren for Inspired Abundance writes, "The more you help others, the more others will want to help you. It never seems to fail. When you're generous, good things just seem to happen. You can never predict the benefits you'll receive." (51) It's just as I said before, when you put positive energy out into the world – or the universe – it finds its way back to you. If you are encouraging others to pay it forward, it may not come back to you immediately, but it may come back to you in the form of good karma. Think of it as the universe balancing itself out and returning the favor for you doing part of its good work.

    Karma speaks to a point that I have brought up repeatedly in this chapter. You have to be helping others for the right reasons.

Why?

    This is because karma does not reward an action; it rewards the intent behind the action. Let me give you an example. You are driving at an approved speed, in a sober state, and you are fully concentrating on the road, yet somehow a pedestrian appears almost from out of nowhere and you hit them. You do your level best to avoid the accident, but there is no time to out-maneuver them as they fall upon your path. You have injured someone, nonetheless, but it was not your intention to do so – and you did everything in your power in that moment to avoid it. Now, if you were to maliciously go looking for someone that you bear a grudge against in order to hit them with your car and make it look accidental, you too have injured someone. Now in which scenario do you think you will be better off – not legally, not emotionally, but in terms of your karma? The same way that the legal system is in place to weigh up the intentions and fault of the person behind the wheel in both of these scenarios, karma does the same. So when you go to help someone with the intention of helping them, you can be assured of creating good karma for yourself. Similarly, when you go to help someone with the intention of getting something out of it, you can be assured of creating bad karma for yourself.

Meditation adviser, Sanjeev Verma writes, "Anytime you put an action in motion with intention that is an act of karma, which, in turn, has consequences. It comes full circle, in some sense, as every action has a reaction." (52) From this we can understand that karma is not a bargaining token, we cannot try to cheat the system. Only genuine intentions will harness good karma. The only way to do this is to not think about the potential of a reward while you are helping others, but genuinely help others for the joy of uplifting another living being. It's not like currency; you cannot tell when it will come back around. All that you can be certain of is that every action that you take, will have a reaction based on your intentions while you were taking it.

Do not attempt to help others in a way that is counterintuitive to your core values. This works out the same way as helping someone with less than pure intentions. When you help others in a way that flows parallel with your own core values you will have a far easier time fulfilling your role as a helper instead of feeling forced to help for the sake of raking up some form of karmic currency. Remember, it does not work that way. Karma does not always come back as a reward right away.

Think of it this way.

Let's say you go out and start helping others. You leave a lasting impact on the people within your community, and you begin to become well known for your charitable nature. The years roll on and one day you close your eyes for the very last time, as we all will. Let's hypothesize that you will have a loved one left behind – a child, a spouse, or anyone that may have been close to you. After your passing, they are down on their luck, but one fine day as fate would have it, your bereaved comes across someone you had once selflessly helped. In their hour of need, your loved one is helped by the very same person that you had once helped. The pay-it-forward chain which I spoke of earlier has now come full circle. Our ego tells us that our lives have to be centered around ourselves, but it is in giving that we truly receive. It is in giving that we leave a lasting legacy. You must remove yourself from your ego so that you can lift the burden of self-centeredness from your shoulders. Acknowledge that what you do today, by living in the present, will come back around in the benefit of your name - just perhaps not while you are around to see it. Maybe it will, and maybe it won't; either way is perfectly fine. All you need to focus on is the here and now.

There are three types of karma that can be at play, namely Sanchitta; Parabda; and Agami. Sanchitta karma is the culmination of past good or bad deeds. It is the actions that you have previously taken without the karma from them having come to be yet. One of these karmas coming to be could be in the form of the person whom you had helped reaching out to help your loved one after you are gone. Parabda is a form of instant karma. It is your current intentions and actions – and the results which they produce for you in your lifetime. Think about your shirt sleeve getting snagged on a door as you attempt to storm out of a room in a fierce mood. Agami karma is linked to the future steps that you take which are directly linked to your current intentions. This can be seen as the successful outcome of your long-term core goal due to the positive steps that you are taking in your life right now. Within this there are also the 12 Laws of Karma, which are all activated when you begin selflessly helping others. You are particularly activating: The Law of Humility; The Law of Growth; The Law of Responsibility; The Law of Connection; The Law of Giving and Hospitality; The Law of Here and Now; The Law of Change; The Law of Patience and Reward; and The Law of Significance and Inspiration. There are very few things in life that can be said to activate all the laws of karma simultaneously and by helping others, you are bound to be living a life of karmic positivity.

When you acknowledge that you cannot control everything and you begin to accept this notion – as you have learned to do in the previous chapter – you are activating the karmic Law of Humility. The universe acknowledges you as someone who has humbled themselves enough to acknowledge they are not in control and you work in the flow of this law instead of against it. As you begin to harness the power of prayer – and become introspective – you are activating the karmic Law of Growth. This growth will be a periodic occurrence. As your environment changes, your self-awareness and its reaction to those changes will lead to growth. By helping others and being mindful of the way in which you treat them, you are activating the karmic Law of Responsibility. The universe will recognize you as someone whom is responsible not only for yourself but for the people around you. As you engage with the people whom you help in a genuine manner, you are activating the karmic Law of Connection. Under this law there is the belief that everything happens for a reason because of the fact that everything in existence is connected in some way or another. Coming to this conclusion further helps you in the process of letting go. You are not able to control this thread that connects us. There will always be ripple effects that are out of your hands. Your job is not to try and control this ripple, but merely to flow with it or ride the wave as it happens. The karmic Law of Giving and Hospitality is activated simply through your selfless acts of giving to others of yourself – whether it's your time or any other resources. Remember to do this with pure intentions and not for some sort of self-righteous bragging rights. When you let go of that which you cannot control, such as something negative from your past, or even what you expect to come of the future - when you actually stop to smell the roses as they say – you are activating the karmic Law of the Here and Now. Living in the moment is the only way to live a fulfilled and balanced life. When you break the cycle of frequenting bars in an attempt to meet someone significant in your life – and you seek other, healthy arenas to do so – you are activating the Law of Change. You are effectively breaking old ways of doing things that have constantly led you to the same unsatisfactory results. When you acknowledge that all great things – such as your long-term goal – take time and you are patient you are activating the karmic Law of Patience and Reward. When you live an inspired life and acknowledge your significance in the thread that connects all of us together, you are activating the karmic Law of Significance and Inspiration. Ultimately, helping others helps you to activate almost all of the karmic or universal laws.

Looking at things from a karmic perspective offers a deep, spiritual insight into living a life in service of others. The reason why I like the idea of karma is that it is broad enough to transcend religion or personal belief, and it offers exemplary evidence of its own existence. There is one more way in which you can help others. Let's have a look at praying for others before we wrap up.

◆ ◆ ◆

In Chapter Three you were made aware of the power of prayer – in whatever form that may be for you. Once you have begun helping others, you can boost the positive impact which you have on their lives by praying for them. Let's get the elephant out of the room before we look at this in a bit more detail. I am not telling you to rush people with the statement "I'm praying for you" or to give out insincere versions of "keeping you in my prayers". Prayer is a divine connection between you and your higher power; you do not need to tell people that you are praying for them for it to work. In fact, you may encounter some people would not appreciate the statement – or the sentiment. Remember that when you help others you are not doing it to brag or broadcast that you have helped them, you are doing it because you genuinely want to help them.

The same goes with prayer.

If you are genuinely praying for someone because you want to help harness a spiritual guidance over their lives you will not feel the need for them to know. It is for you and your higher power to know. Prayer can also give you the clarity needed to help others. This mental alignment of positive self-talk allows your conscience to search for and manifest ways in which you can help someone. Perhaps as your mind was reeling over someone's situation you didn't have the right capacity to help them or to even comment on their situation – whatever that may be. However, as you quietly reflect on their situation and seek to broaden your own capacity, you may find that you can creatively assist them in traversing a difficult moment in their lives.

Now, if you wish to help someone unlock the benefits of prayer just as you have done, it is very important to approach them gently. Prayer is a very personal, and sometimes sensitive, subject. If you feel that someone in your life is ready for you to speak to them about the power of prayer, mention it to them. If they are reluctant to discuss how they can unlock their potential through prayer, there is no need to push them into the conversation – you would only be pushing them away and hardening their heart. However, if they are receptive to the notion of prayer, explain it to them as I have explained it to you, and if you so choose, recommend they read Chapter Three of this book in particular. By sharing the techniques which you have gained through this book you are helping someone to unlock their own potential. You are also increasing your connectedness to someone who shares the same values as you do. Please be weary of how you interpret this. I am not saying that a praying man and a non-praying man cannot connect at a deep level. Nor am I saying that in order for you to help someone, you need to share a belief system or core values. What I am saying is that you can help others by sharing your knowledge and boosting your connectedness to both those with similar and different values from your own. It all comes down to communication and your graciousness to accept a no – as well as your openness to share when you receive a yes.

Let's get back to praying for others now. I have mentioned how your belief in your prayer, as well as in your higher power, will determine the outcome of your journey, but let's look at it from the perspective of someone else's journey. Let's tie this in with karma as well. Your belief in the power of prayer can have profound positive effects on someone else's life. By praying for others, you are sowing the seeds for the 12 Laws of Karma to be activated – because this is also a form of helping others, just on a spiritual level instead of a physical one. Remember your higher power is not a genie. Prayer works through positivity. I don't want anyone to despair over the idea of someone praying for ill will over your life. Prayer simply does not work that way – and anyone putting that negative energy out into the universe will surely see that negativity reflected back to them. Prayer is about love – for one's self and for others. It should invoke positivity. Anything else is just negative wishful thinking that will not come to fruition over anyone else's life but the person thinking of it to begin with.

The next time you engage in prayer I want you to do so with positivity, pure intentions and with helping someone else in mind. Not only will you be creating positivity for your own life, but you could spiritually assist someone in unlocking their own potential. By now, you know that I always offer a scientific approach – as well as a spiritual approach – to everything. Let's keep with this theme and have a look towards Sir Isaac Newton for some inspiration as we move forward in this final section of hyper-goal setting for lifelong success.

◆ ◆ ◆

Famed physicist, Sir Isaac Newton, puts it perfectly as per his third law of motion: "Every action must have an equal and opposite reaction." In order for you to take the action of helping others, you must acknowledge that being involved in their lives could lead to you repelling others from your own life. Perhaps they have been less than healthy for your mental and emotional wellbeing. This is an example of you going into other people's lives while some of the people in your own life exit it. Your action leads to an equal and opposite reaction. In this sense helping others will be the wind which lifts your balloon up. Your newfound positive nature will equally repel those of a negative nature from you who may have been weighing you – and therefore your balloon – down. Everything that you put out into the universe through your dreams, imagination, prayer and actions in helping others will all have a reaction. Things always find a way to come full circle.

Trust in the process.

◆ ◆ ◆

Let's recap the stage of Helping Others before concluding. By this stage, you have mastered the art of letting go of full control over your dream. You've put it out into the universe, or to your higher power, and you are happily getting on with your daily affirmations. You are focusing on living a fulfilled and balanced life. It is now time to add value to this balance. Living a life of purpose and in service of others is something that we should all strive to do. I want you to embrace the idea of helping others. Don't let extrinsic motivators be your main guide at this stage. Allow intrinsic motivation and the joys of paying it forward to guide you as to how you should help others.

When you have helped others, be gracious about it. Don't expect anything in return; instead encourage them to pay it forward. Paying it forward is the act of passing on the kindness that someone has shown you instead of working towards returning the favor. This frees the person whom you have helped from the pressure of returning the favor to you, and opens them up to the joy of helping someone else. Fostering this sense of giving and connectedness not only uplifts your own spirit, but triggers a chain of events that could come back to you in the most positive way.

When you live a life in service of others, it serves as a great source of fulfillment and motivation. Not only this, but it serves as a healthy alternative to the distractions which we fill our lives with. Have you ever been feeling a little stressed out and you immediately pick up your phone and scroll through social media to numb your mind and pass the time? The problem with technological distraction is that constantly being on social media can compound your feelings of stress. Getting out and helping others removes you from the incessant buzz of technology and allows you to engage in meaningful interactions.

If you have ever been in a fierce mood, making your general demeanor towards others less than kind at the time, you may have gone on to experience instant karma. In one of those moments, have you ever tried to storm out of a room only for your shirt or jacket sleeve to get caught on the door handle on the way out? This can be seen as a form of instant karma. Now karma is not always instantaneous, sometimes it takes a while to roll back around – but it does come back around. Focus on sowing the seeds of good karma and activating its 12 Laws.

Once you have begun helping others, you can boost the positive impact which you have on their lives by praying for them. Remember that when you help others you are not doing it to brag or broadcast that you have helped them, you are doing it because you genuinely want to help them. The same goes with prayer. If you are genuinely praying for someone because you want to help harness a spiritual guidance over their lives you will not feel the need for them to know. It is for you and your higher power to know. Prayer can also give you the clarity needed to help others. This mental alignment of positive self-talk allows your conscience to search for and manifest ways in which you can help someone. It's all about using the moment of prayer to reflect on how you can further help someone.

Famed physicist, Sir Isaac Newton, puts it perfectly as per his third law of motion: "Every action must have an equal and opposite reaction." In order for you to take the action of helping others, you must acknowledge that being involved in their lives could lead to you repelling others from your own life. Perhaps they have been less than healthy for your mental and emotional wellbeing. This is an example of you going into other people's lives while some of the people in your own life exit it. Your action leads to an equal and opposite reaction. Everything that you put out into the universe through your dreams, imagination, prayer and actions in helping others will all have a reaction.

◆ ◆ ◆

Allow me to leave you with one final story. *In the winter of 2011, I had been attending a company party. It was a good night. We all got to unwind, connect and laugh the evening away. While it was an enjoyable evening, I had begun feeling a bit financially trapped in this company, and I had already spent months looking for alternative employment – unbeknownst to everyone there. I had decided to enjoy myself, but I couldn't put my dissatisfaction out of my mind. By the time most of us who were in attendance had left, it was quite late in the evening. I made my usual trip home. I had made this trip every single day. I knew the road, the sights and the sounds.*

This night was different.

I made my final turn on to my street, and I could barely make out three figures in the distance. I glanced down at the clock. "What are people doing out in the cold at this time of night?" I had thought to myself.

As I got closer, my heart sank. A mother and her two young children were sitting outside the entrance to one of the houses on my street. The children couldn't have been older than three and seven years old respectively. I slowed down, and drove close enough for them to hear me. I asked her what she was doing out on the street in the dead of night. It was freezing out. I asked her if she was in need of assistance. The woman explained to me how she had travelled all day with her two young children from a town in the east of the country. She had come to Tehran to seek treatment at a specialized orthopedic hospital. She had been suffering from severe pain in her back and her knee, and I couldn't have imagined what the cold must have been doing to her aching bones that night. I said that I understood, but went on to ask if she had not arranged a place to stay. She replied that she had indeed arranged a place to stay. This house which she was sitting in front of belonged to a relative of hers, but they were not home. With no phone of her own, and no money – just an address written on a crumpled piece of paper – she had no way of contacting them and she did not know the area at all. My heart sank. I looked into her tired eyes and I could see the pain, fear and frustration on her face. I look down at these little children, shivering and huddling up close to their mother for warmth. Seeing that is enough to make a grown man cry. I pulled myself together and immediately counted all the money which I had on me, explaining that there was a motel not too far from here. I offered to take them there, but she was so overjoyed at the help and insisted that she couldn't put me out of my way. I quickly wrote down the address to my office and gave it to her – asking her to come and see me at noon the following day.

 I drove home with a heavy heart, filled with worry for this woman and her children. I made my way to bed and finally fell into a deep sleep. The next day, my worry for her consumed my mind the entire morning at the office. Around noon, I received a call from the front desk, telling me that a woman and two young children were in the lobby waiting for me. It was such a huge relief. I made my way to the lobby as quickly as I could and I was greeted by three smiling faces which seemed a world away from the fear and sadness which I had seen displayed on them just a few hours before. She thanked me profusely, and I was happy to learn that she had received the treatment *and medication which she desperately needed for her condition. We spoke briefly and the children weaved around us – playing so merrily as if nothing had happened just the night before. I bid them farewell and they made their journey back home.*

I walked back up to my office and sat down, feeling grateful that I had been in the right place at the right time to help this woman. In the moment that she had needed my help that previous evening, I was no longer thinking about my own issues. My only focus was the safety and wellbeing of this stranger and her children. Some weeks went by and to my surprise I finally had a breakthrough in my own life. I received a very generous job offer and for some reason my mind was instantly taken back to that night out in the cold. I remembered the woman and her children. I never fully understood why until I was told by a friend later that these two events were definitely related. I laughed at first, but I began thinking back to occurrences which were similar to this. Moments in time where I had been compelled to help a fellow human being – and how helping them had managed to make me completely forget all of my own problems; to focus solely on them.

This has been a repetitive theme throughout my life as I have begun working from a place of more deep internal gratitude. Whenever you find it in your heart to help someone even in your own time of need; you will always be inviting positive energy back into your life. Today I completely acknowledge this magical thread that connects all of our actions and thoughts, as well as how we conduct ourselves with one another. Every time you think that your actions won't make an impact, tell yourself that everything happens for a reason. Sometimes we are meant to receive the blessings, and sometimes we are meant to be a blessing for others. We are all intricately connected to one another.

◆ ◆ ◆

As we conclude this journey of hyper-goal setting for lifelong success, I think you have come to realize that your ultimate goal should be to live a stress-reduced and fulfilling life.

Whatever your goal may be, you only have this one life to live – live it to the fullest. Embrace your dreams with arms wide open; envision them, define them; pray over them – but don't let them consume you. Be willing to trust in the process enough for you to take your focus off of your long-term goal. Let it go and it will eventually come to be. All that is meant for you is already yours; you just have to manifest it. Once you align yourself within this growth mindset, you will be able to add value to your own life and the lives of others by helping them where you can and praying for clarity where you can't.

Live presently.
Live with intention.
Live your purpose.

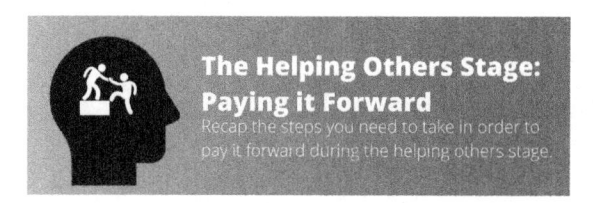

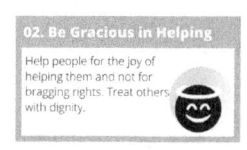

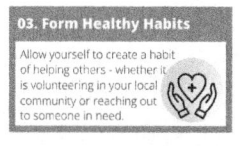

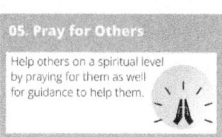

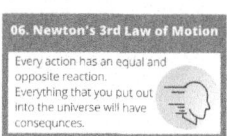

The Helping Others Stage: Paying it Forward

Recap the steps you need to take in order to pay it forward during the helping others stage.

01. Add Value to Your Life
Add value to your life by giving back to others and paying-it-forward.

02. Be Gracious in Helping
Help people for the joy of helping them and not for bragging rights. Treat others with dignity.

03. Form Healthy Habits
Allow yourself to create a habit of helping others - whether it is volunteering in your local community or reaching out to someone in need.

04. Sow Seeds of Good Karma
Activate all 12 Laws of Good Karma by helping others selflessly.

05. Pray for Others
Help others on a spiritual level by praying for them as well for guidance to help them.

06. Newton's 3rd Law of Motion
Every action has an equal and opposite reaction. Everything that you put out into the universe will have consequnces.

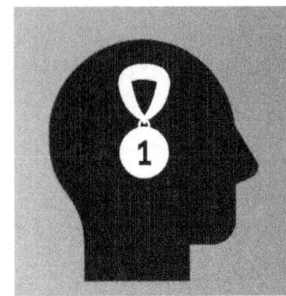

Hyper-Goal Setting for Lifelong Success

01. Dream
Dream without boundaries. This is not the place to play it safe. Dream of your deepest desires.

02. Imagine
Use your imagination to define your vision. Be as creative as you can be as you start to detail your dream.

03. Pray
Pray with gratitude for that which you are yet to receive. Whether you believe in a deity, the universe or your own higher consciousness - pray.

04. Let it Go
You cannot breathe life into something by holding on to it so tightly that you begin to choke the life out of it. Let it go so that it can manifest.

05. Help Others
Align your core values with your activities. Pay-it-forward and volunteer within your community. Your connectivity will help you succeed.

ABOUT THE AUTHOR

Who is Mohsen Zargaran?

Mohsen Zargaran was born in November of 1977 in Isfahan City, Iran. Isfahan is a city with a rich history at the heart of the Persian Empire. In 1979, just two years after Mohsen's birth, Naqsh-e Jahan Square, also known as the Royal Square, was designated as a UNESCO World Heritage Site.
While Mohsen's true birth date is in November, his father had arranged to have his birth date changed to September so that he could begin his schooling journey a year earlier.

Born to a middle class family, Mohsen's father had a job working in the Ministry of Agriculture in the government sector and his mother was a devoted home-maker; taking care of Mohsen, his two elder sisters, and their household with love and pride.

1978 saw the beginning of the Iranian revolution, which lasted a year and resulted in the toppling of the monarchy. The throws of unemployed youth, as well as thousands from religious schools took to the streets to protest the lavish life led by the monarch in the face of growing disparity. Mohsen remembers this only from the stories his family have told him; he was only two months old when it all began.

In 1980, Iraq invaded Iran and a war ensued that went on for eight years. Those are the years that he remembers all too clearly. As a young boy, he would have to carry a dampened towel in his backpack at all times as a measure of caution should there have been an event of chemical bombing. He recalls the years where each family was assigned a quota for necessities such as milk, meat, cooking oil, sugar, rice and fuel. Practically everything had a quota during those years. He spent many a cold winter day shivering in the long lines to receive his family's two bottles of milk as part of their weekly quota. As a small and shy boy, he was often jostled along the line, and bullied out of his space by some of the elder men. His childhood was spent in turmoil, but it is this turmoil - amidst his most formidable years - that has led to his ability to view the world with optimism. The warm, nurturing love of his family has allowed him to grow up into a man who operates from a place of deep inner strength.

◆ ◆ ◆

Summer was the greatest time of the year for Mohsen. He spent his days exploring and trying to discover as much as he could about the world around him. With his home-made microscope in hand, he would study all kinds of insects and plant matter that he would come across. He fondly remembers how he enjoyed sitting along the pond in their backyard and dipping his feet in; wading through the soft sand to see what other discoveries he could rustle up.

He was a curious child who always wondered how the universe worked, and what the meaning was behind it all. He wondered how things happened in the physical and metaphysical plain; how we were all created; and how people might have lived centuries ago. He toyed with the notion of being able to read other people, and perhaps even read their minds, as well as how to make a change in the world. His thoughts would sometimes dishearten him; thinking that there was nothing left in the world to invent, and that anything worth creating had already been created. He had a mental turning point when he came to the idea that every single person in this world has a unique capacity within themselves and a mission to accomplish. He believed that each person's unique capacity was predestined for them, and only them, and that if even one person were to break from their mission, there would be no other person to fill the gap they would leave behind. In essence, he believed that we all have a purpose.

◆ ◆ ◆

When Mohsen completed his high school education, he went on to study Telecommunications Engineering at Isfahan University of Technology; moving on to land his first job as an engineer with a local telecom company in 2001 – the very same year that he was happily wed. His strong work ethic and dedication saw him quickly moving on to work for the well-known telecommunications company, Siemens, in 2004; before moving on to the telecom giant, Nokia, in 2005. He climbed Nokia's corporate ladder and went on to become their Program Manager and then their Account Manager in Tehran. However, this steady climb was not without heartache, and Mohsen went through an emotionally devastating experience. Jump forward to just two years after this experience, and he felt that it had led him to what he has termed: "a soul awakening" in April of 2009. This began his journey into the man that he is today. He was a determined young man; earning a Business Administration Diploma from the University of Tehran in 2011. In 2012, Mohsen and his wife filed for separation, but he would remain a dedicated father to their son. From there, he prepared to make his move to an Iranian founded company in an Executive Level position in 2013. In 2014 Mohsen re-married, and would go on to have a second-born son and a daughter. He would eventually earn his Master's in Economics in 2015.

2017 was the year that Mohsen became the National Business Head of Samsung Electronics; and following the trend set during his days with Nokia, he received many accolades from his employers.

In 2020 Mohsen took the bold initiative to move to Canada in order to pursue his life and career there. He has been focused on quenching his childhood thirst for knowledge; constantly reading, and taking skills courses. He has thus far obtained certificates pertaining to project management, coaching, and the signature program of The 7 Habits of Highly Effective People, to name but a few. He is currently focusing on his passion of helping others achieve their goals; as well as conducting business consulting and executive coaching.

◆ ◆ ◆

Mohsen began his journey to becoming the self-help and inspirational coach that he is today by helping friends and colleagues who were seeking a better life. He spent countless hours being a shoulder upon which they could lay their burdens, and worked with them on finding positive solutions to their problems. He has always been of the mindset that self-awareness is of great importance. Learning about the laws that govern our universe paired with a willingness and openness to change, is the very first step to removing yourself from a place of mental suffering, and on to a place of happiness and fulfilment. Try as anyone may, unless the person in question is open to change, nothing anyone else does for them will matter.

◆ ◆ ◆

From The Author

My wish is for my book to reach millions of people and to help them change their lives for the better. I hope it plays a role in reconnecting them with their souls and reaching their goals. My aim is to help as many people live a life without stress and fear - to help them live limitlessly.
It is possible.

GLOSSARY

12 Laws of Karma: These 12 laws include: The Great Law; The Law of Creation; The Law of Humility; The Law of Growth; The Law of Responsibility; The Law of Connection; The Law of Force; The Law of Giving and Hospitality; The Law of Here and Now; The Law of Change; The Law of Patience and Reward; The Law of Significance and Inspiration.
Agami: Future actions that result from your present actions.
Audial learner: Someone who learns best via auditory media such as music, speech and sound.
Cathartic: Psychological relief.
Crypto currency: A digital currency in which encryption is used.
Day trade: The process of trading on the stock market in which a trader buys and sells stocks in the same day.
Extrinsic motivators: Any external source of motivation such as financial gain.
Faux ceiling: False or fake ceiling. Limitations which we place on ourselves.
Fight-or-flight: The acute stress response to a perceived survival threat.
Human libraries: Sources of information. The notion of people being human libraries is relatively new concept that can allow you to garner information via the experiences of others.
Hyper-goals: The series of goals which follow your main, or core, long-term goal.
Inertia: The tendency to do nothing. A propensity to remain unchanged.

Intrinsic motivators: Internal sources of motivation such as a passion towards doing something.
Karma: The sum of your actions which has the potential to dictate your fate.
Kinesthetic learner: A person who has to be immersed in an activity, or subject, in order to learn from it.
Long-term goals: These are five or more years into the future.
Manifestation: The process of harnessing that which is already in existence.
Mantra: A statement to live by or to use during meditation and/or prayer.
Metaphysical: Transcendental or spiritual.
Mid-term goals: Goals that are anywhere from 6 months to 3 years into the future.
Other-imposed self-fulfilling prophecy: The opinions which others have of you coming to be due to your belief in their opinion.
Parabda: All of one's past karma which can be presently experienced.
Pay it forward: The process of paying the kindness someone has shown you forward to someone else, instead of paying it back.
Placebo effect: A psychological phenomena whereby one's belief in a treatment will have significant positive effects in the treatment of said person.
Positive affirmation: A repetitive positive statement which you can use in prayer or when engaging in self-talk.
Prefrontal cortex: The part of the human brain responsible for complex cognitive behavior, decision making and moderating mood and behavior.
Pristine moment: A moment whereby one is able to engage in reflective behavior such addressing one's own conscience and speaking to it.
Reciprocity: A mutually beneficial exchange.
Sanchitta: This is the karma that you will not receive in this life.
Self-fulfilling prophecy: is phenomena whereby something

which you put out into the universe comes to be.

Self-imposed self-fulfilling prophecy: Your belief in a prophecy over your life which takes you through the actions that leads to the fruition of that prophecy.

Self-talk: Engaging with one's own conscience during a pristine moment.

Sound shadow: The disturbance of sound waves as an object passes between you and external sounds.

Status quo: The existing way of doing things.

Supernatural: Anything outside the realm of scientific explanation.

Toman: Iranian currency.

Vision board: A creative installation depicting a goal and the surrounding emotions, motives and other pertinent factors.

Visual learner: A person who learns via this use of visual cues such as text, imagery and video.

Visualization: The process of seeing something which has not yet come to pass.

Whiplash: The after effects of a high impact situation such as a car accident.

BIBLIOGRAPHY

1,2,3) Locke, T. (2020). Why Spanx founder Sara Blakely hid her billion-dollar business idea from friends and family for a year. CNBC, Make It.

4) Dearborn, Edwin. (2019). Achieving your goals, Aristotle's Insights. Edwin Dearborn Website.

5) Connor, Julie Ph.D. (2014). 7 Reasons why it's crucial to have a dream. Dr. Julie Connor Website.

6) Barr, Corbett. (2009). How to Create a Vision for Your Life. Corbett Barr. Corbett Barr Website.

7) Zimmerman, Angelina. (2016). 13 Incredible Facts to Help You Unleash the Power of Your Mind. Zimmerman, Angelina. Inc.com.

8) Hurlburt, Russell T Ph.D. (2011). Not Everyone Conducts Inner Speech. Psychology Today.

9) Hume, David. (1739). A Treatise of Human Nature. Gutenberg Files.

10) Kruse, Kevin. (2017). Dream Big: If Your Goals Don't Scare You, They're Too Small. Forbes Online.

11) Jones, Clifford. (2016). The Power of Dreaming Big. Biz Journals.

12) Melnick, Lloyd. (2018). The risk of status quo bias. Lloyd Melnick Website.

13) Imatge, Zuluoaga. (2013). Albert Einstein : "Insanity is doing the same thing over and over again and expecting different results." Dicere Global.

14) Goddard, Neville. (2007). The Resurrection. Devorss & Co.
15) Goddard, Neville. (2010). The Power of Awareness. Pacific Publishing Studio.
16) Baumgartner, Jennifer. (2011). Visualize It. Psychology Today.
17) Baumgartner, Jennifer. (2011). Visualize It. Psychology Today.
18) Ducey, Jake. (2019). How To Manifest Your Life Using Your Imagination. Jake Ducey Blog.
19) Ducey, Jake. (2019). How To Manifest Your Life Using Your Imagination. Jake Ducey Blog.
20) Ewer, Tom. (2011). If You Believe You Can Succeed, You're Already Half Way There. Leaving Work Behind.
21) Canalichio, Pete. (2017). Envisioning Success Is Your Best First Step to Making Your Dreams a Reality. Entrepreneur Online.
22) Popova, Maria. (2014). Fixed vs. Growth: The Two Basic Mindsets That Shape Our Lives. Brain Pickings.
23) St Louis, Molly. (2017) How to Spot Visual, Auditory, and Kinesthetic-Learning Executives. If your great ideas are being overlooked, perhaps it's time to communicate them differently. Inc.com.
24) Christian, Lyn. (2019). How to Define and Achieve your long term goals. Soul Salt.
25) Christian, Lyn. (2019). How to Define and Achieve your long term goals. Soul Salt.
26) Newsome, Teresa. (2016). 11 Sneaky Ways Relationships Can Slow Your Goals. Bustle.
27) Handel, Steven. (2013). The Power of Foresight: Why Looking Into the Future is the Key to Success. The Emotion Machine.
28) Haseltine, Eric Ph.D. (2015). Yes, You Have a Sixth Sense, and You Should Trust It. Psychology Today.
29) Vidal, Guillermo. (2018). Your Connection to the Creative Force of the Universe is Proof there is a Higher Power at Work in

Your Life. Medium.

30) Entheo Nation. (2019). Manifest Faster through The Power of Alignment. Entheo Nation.

31) Sasson, Remez. (2020). The Power of Faith and Belief. Success Consciousness.

32) Eggen, John. (2020). Tap into THIS before writing your book. John Eggen LinkedIn Article.

33) Babauta, Leo. (2016). Exclusive Interview: Stephen Covey on His Morning Routine, Blogs, Technology, GTD and The Secret. Zen habits.

34) Bathie, Emma. (2017). Are you in Energetic Alignment with Your Goals. GoalCast.

35) Cherry, Kendra. (2020). How the Placebo Effect Works in Psychology. Very Well Mind.

36) Rogers, Kristen. (2020). The psychological benefits of prayer: What science says about the mind-soul connection. Edition.

37) Rogers, Kristen. (2020). The psychological benefits of prayer: What science says about the mind-soul connection. Edition.

38) Muir, Tina. (2017). Are You Obsessed With Your Goals? That is Why You Never Reach it. Tina Muir Website.

39) Cunningham, Jamie. (2019). To Achieve Your Goals, You Have to Let Go of Them. Sales Up.

40) Pietrangelo, Ann and Watson, Stephanie. (2020). The Effects of Stress on Your Body. Medically reviewed by Timothy J. Legg, Ph.D, PsyD, CRNP, ACRN, CPH. Healthline.

41) Carpenter, Jess. (2019). How to set short-term goals for greater success in life. Ideapod.

42) Carpenter, Jess. (2019). How to set short-term goals for greater success in life. Ideapod.

43) Tempesta, Daniela. (2013). Why You Should Stop Comparing Yourself to Others. Huffpost.

44) Dixit, Jay. (2008) The Art of Now: Six Steps to Living in the Moment. Psychology Today.

45) Stainton, Bill. (2020). Why Long-Term Planning Doesn't

Work. Bill Stainton Website.

46) Santi, Jenny. (2020). The Secret to Happiness is Helping Others. Time.

47) Pogosyan, Marianna Ph.D. In Helping Others Your Help Yourself. Psychology Today.

48) Cole, Bianca Miller. (2019). 10 Reasons Why Networking Is Essential For Your Career.

49) Tsvetkova, Milena and Macy, Michael. (2014). The Science of 'Paying It Forward'. NY Times.

50) Goz Around. (2016). 5 REASONS WHY YOU SHOULD VOLUNTEER AS A COUPLE. Goz Around.

51) Warren, Hugh. (2017). How Sharing Your Time and Money Helps You Attract More Abundance Into Your Life. Inspired Abundance.

52) Verma, Sanjeev. (2018). 4 Things You Didn't Know About Karma (and How to Make it Work for You). Sonima.

H:1 a) Help.org Drug Abuse Hotline.
https://www.help.org/drug-abuse-hotline/

H:1 b) Canadian Center on Substance Use and Addiction.
https://www.ccsa.ca/addictions-treatment-helplines-canada

Printed in Great Britain
by Amazon